THE HOCKEY
TRIVIA BOOK

THE HOCKEY TRIVIA BOOK

BRUCE C. COOPER
GENE HART

LEISURE PRESS

NEW YORK

A publication of Leisure Press
597 Fifth Avenue, New York, NY 10017
©1984 by Bruce C. Cooper and Eugene C. Hart
All rights reserved. Printed in the U.S.A.

Library of Congress Cataloging in Publication Data

Cooper, Bruce.
  The hockey trivia book.

  1. Hockey—Miscellanea. I. Hart, Gene. II. Title.
GV847.C62 1984   796.96's   84-757
ISBN 0-88011-233-6

Book Design: David Hebenstreit
Cover Design: Debbie Silverman
Typeset by: Lewis Publishing, Oakland, CA.

Cover Slide Courtesy of the Philadelphia Flyers

ACKNOWLEDGMENTS

Before we get started, we would like to acknowledge with thanks a number of folks who have supplied us with support and advice, aided us in our research, supplied information and photographs and otherwise assisted us as we put together our little compendium of hockey "trivia" for you. We tip our Mikita helmets in no particular order to: Frank Mathers, President of the AHL Hershey Bears and one of the true "gentlemen" in hockey; Steve Summers, resident shinny scribe of the Harrisburg *Patriot-News;* Gordie Anziano, VP and raconteur of the American Hockey League; Bill Adler, Central Hockey League Vice President and official sage; referee Ron Wicks; Edmonton broadcaster and former keeper of the Philadelphia Firebirds, Gregg Pilling; Hall of Fame Curator - and keeper of the Stanley Cup - M.H. "Lefty" Reid; Jim Cnockaert and Pete Maxwell of the Port Huron (MI) *Times-Herald*; our favorite Buffalo Sabre, Taro Tsujimoto; La Salle College sports informer Frank Bertucci; Mike "Il Voce" Emrick, Ph.D., of the New Jersey Devils; Jack Button of the Washington Capitals (our expert on Latin goalies); and the following NHL PR personages - Jeanne Dennis (Hartford), Larry Rubin and Mark Piazza (Philadelphia), Janet Halligan (New York Rangers), and Scott Carmichael (Los Angeles). We also thank former Philadelphia Blazers (WHA) and Firebirds (NAHL) broadcaster John McAdams for several vertical lines down the middle of the page. To all we express our sincere thanks, and hope each finds a question in this book that he or she can answer!

TABLE OF CONTENTS

Introduction   8

I.

"Bingo," "Battleship" & "Boom-Boom" — Ice Chips I   11
Answers   15
Super Question ONE — "Who is that NHL'er from . . .
    Big Spring, Texas?"   18
Answers   21

II.

"All In The Family" . . .
Hockey's Fathers, Sons & Brothers   23
Answers   26
Super Question TWO — Great Forward Lines . . .
    When Three is MORE than One   31
Answers   34

III.

Of Penalties, Shots & Penalty Shots . . . NHL Rules   35
Answers   39
Super Question THREE — Birds, Bees & Bears . . .
    Hockey Team Logos   43
Answers   51

IV.

Arenas . . . The "Temples" of Hockey   57
Answers   60
Super Question FOUR —
    "You mean that's not his REAL name?!"   67
Answers   70

V.

"Canada, United States, Soviet Union and . . ."
Ice Chips II   71
Answers   75
Super Question FIVE — From 16 to 68 . . .
    The NHL's Youngest & Oldest   78
Answers   81

VI.

"Minnesota Drafts . . . The Governor" . . . The WHA 83
Answers 87
Super Question SIX — "Do you recall . . .
   the WHA's FIRST All-Stars?" 93
Answers 95

VII.

"Dad, why are they called 'targets'?" . . . Goalies 97
Super Question SEVEN — Hockey's MOST Exclusive Team . . .
   The NHL's Retired Numbers 107
Answers 109

VIII.

"And the winner is . . ." . . . Hockey Trophies 113
Answers 118
Super Question EIGHT — "What do Nick Fotiu. . .
   and Al Abour have in common? 123
Answers 125

IX.

"Big Horns," "Buckaroos" & "Bluebirds"
   — Ice Chips III 131
Answers 138
Photo Identification Answers 141
About The Authors 142

INTRODUCTION

Our Websters (well actually our Funk & Wagnalls) defines "trivia" as: "Unimportant matters; trifles." We beg to differ. While sports "trivia" may not be the most important aspect of our pastimes, it seems to us that it *does* play a key role in giving sport its vitality. Hockey trivia is what gives our favorite sport its humanity. It is the life's blood of hockey lore, and more often than not provides a few laughs as well. And that we find difficult to dismiss as "unimportant matters" or "trifles." If you have picked up this book, you already agree.

Both you and we have seen many "trivia books" as we have followed sports, and we find that most of them suffer from a similar fault. They are basically "fact oriented," i.e., "Who scored the most shorthanded goals in the 1939-40 season for the EAHL McIntyre Miners?" It may be trivia, but not the kind of thing that sticks in your mind. We decided on a different approach. Most of our questions first establish what we hope you will find to be an interesting and novel premise which you may not have thought of before. Then we pose our question based on that premise which we hope you will find both interesting and thought provoking. You will find that in most cases our answers are considerably longer than our questions. We try to tell you a little story with many of them and hope that your reaction will be, "Hum, I didn't know *that!*" We hope you will then add these little bits of hockey trivia to your collection of working knowledge of the game—and use them to stump your friends.

You will find questions of three different basic types in this book. The first type is in nine chapters averaging about fifteen questions each on various topics of hockey trivia, i.e., Arenas, Trophies, Hockey Families, Rules, Goalies, the WHA, and three chapters of miscellaneous questions we call "Ice Chips." The second type is our eight "Super Questions." These are multi-part questions which delve much deeper into your knowledge of particular areas of the game. They are meant to be both challenging and entertaining, and to provide you with more "meaty" trivia. Our third challenge is to identify twenty-six current or recent NHL GMs, head coaches or assistant coaches whose pictures appear throughout the book. The pictures of them were taken early in each man's professional hockey career while he was a player in the minor leagues.

These twenty-six NHL personalities are shown in photographs **(Mystery Player A-Z)** throughout the book. The identities of these NHL general managers, head coaches and assistant coaches are located near the end of the book. Good Luck!

You will also find that we have made a conscious effort to give the "other" leagues of hockey their due in our book. While the NHL is certainly well represented, you will also find references to many other circuits such as the AHL, CHL, IHL, WHL, OHA, WCHL, QMJHL, OHL, EPHL, CPHL, SHL, NAHL, ACHL, NEHL, WCHA, ECAC, NCAA and AJHL. And of course we have included quite a bit about the World Hockey Association (WHA) which is a treasure trove of trivia all by itself.

We hope you will find our little look back into the trivia of hockey both entertaining and instructional, and will agree that "trifles" are indeed important.

Enjoy.

Bruce C. Cooper
Gene Hart

PART I

"BINGO," "BATTLESHIP" & "BOOM-BOOM" . . . ICE CHIPS I

To start you off, we open with the first of the three sections throughout the book we call "Ice Chips." Here you will find questions on many different areas of the game of ice hockey. Some are "serious," but many are of a lighter vein. We hope that you will find them interesting.

1 Nicknames in hockey flow like hot water from a Zamboni in hockey. In fact many nicknames end up attached to *more* than one person. We list below eighteen such nicknames that have been given to two or more NHL figures over the years. How many of their owners can you recall?

A. Bingo	J. Ace
B. Battleship	K. Butch
C. Boom-Boom	L. Turk
D. Chief	M. Moose
E. Red	N. Cowboy
F. Babe	O. Busher
G. Rat	P. Punch
H. Rock	Q. Cat
I. Dutch	R. Whitey

2 When Gordie Howe returned to the NHL as a member of the Hartford Whalers for the 1979-80 season, he became the first player to perform on the ice in league play *after* he had been elected to the Hockey Hall of Fame. He was not, however, the only Hall of Famer to appear on the ice in an NHL game that season. Who was the other?

3 What singular honor has the NHL bestowed on In Glas Co, Viceroy Manufacturing Co., and Superior Fabricators Co.?

4 What unusual, if unofficial, record did Flyer defenseman Brad Marsh set in the 1981-82 season that was previously established by Philadelphia winger Ross Lonsberry ten years earlier?

5 In 1967 the NHL doubled its size from six to twelve clubs. Who were the six original coaches named to guide the 1967 *expansion* teams?

6 Now that you have the expansion coaches, who were the six men behind the benches of the six *original* NHL clubs when the 1967-68 season opened?

7 In the years since the 1967 expansion, fourteen other cities have iced NHL teams either with new or transferred franchises. What were those fourteen clubs, what year did each first play in the NHL, and who was the first coach of each?

8 Who was the first player to score 200 goals with a 1967 expansion team?

9 Of the twenty-one current member cities in the NHL, six have been previously represented in the league by earlier teams. What are those six current member cities, what were the names of the NHL clubs that operated in them previously, and in what seasons did they play in the league?

10 What special experience in the background of long-time NHL President Clarence S. Campbell's distinguished public service career could be said to have been especially helpful to him during his administration of the league in the more violent days of hockey in the 50's, 60's and 70's?

11 Trades are a fact of life in sports, and most players are traded at least once during their careers. Occasionally a player is traded twice during a single season, but only once in NHL history has a player been moved within the league *three* times during a single campaign. Who was this much-traveled man, what four NHL clubs did he play for that season, and what "ironic" curiosity about his final move of the season gave him the last laugh on his three previous clubs?

12 Virtually every member of the Hockey Hall of Fame has been associated with the NHL in one way or another, but a few have not. One, in fact, made his name in hockey not in North America at all, but in the Soviet Union. Who is he?

13 What three professional major league hockey teams, active since 1967, have worn skates colored: a) Blue & Gold; b) Green & Gold; and c) Snow White?

14 Most referees and linesmen start off in the game as players and then decide for one reason or another to become officials. One such man was Hall of Fame referee Bill "Big Whistle" Chadwick who was a promising young player with the New York Rovers in the mid-1930's when he retired to become an on-ice official. What unusual reason did he have for making this change in his hockey career?

15 What unusual NHL record did winger Al Hill set with the Philadelphia Flyers on February 14, 1977?

MYSTERY PLAYER A

ICE CHIPS I . . . ANSWERS

1 We have come up with forty-eight current or former NHL figures who have been known by one of our eighteen nicknames at some point in their careers. Here they are:

A. BINGO—Rudolph Kampman, Keith Allen

B. BATTLESHIP—J. Bob Kelly, Albert Leduc

B. BOOM-BOOM—Bernie Geoffrion, Alain Caron

D. CHIEF—Bobby Taylor, Jim Neilson, John Bucyk, Reggie Leach, George Armstrong

E. RED—Gordon Berenson, George Sullivan, Billy Hay, Leonard Kelly, Mervyn Dutton, George Horner

F. BABE—Walter Pratt, Albert Seibert, Cecil Dye

G. RAT—Ken Linseman, Harry Westwick

H. ROCK—Larry Zeidel, Tony Camazzola

I. DUTCH—Earl Reibel, Wilbert Hiller, Frank Nighbor

J. ACE—Garnet Bailey, Irvine Bailey

K. BUTCH—Robert Goring, Pierre Bouchard

L. TURK—Derek Sanderson, Walter Broda, Jim Evers

M. MOOSE—Andre Dupont, Elmer Vasko

N. COWBOY—Bill Flett, Edward Convey

O. BUSHER—Floyd Curry, Harvey Jackson

P. PUNCH—George Imlach, Harry Broadbent

Q. CAT—Emile Francis, John Gagnon, Frederick R. Williams

R. WHITEY—Juha Widing, Bob Clarke, Pat Stapleton

2 NHL Supervisor of Officials Frank Udvari, a Hall of Fame referee, took over for an injured Dave Newell during a game at Nassau Coliseum on December 30, 1979 and finished it in fine style. It was his first on-ice appearance since 1966. He was elected to the Hall of Fame in 1973.

3 These three companies are the only manufacturers of "official NHL" pucks.

4 Brad Marsh was acquired from the Calgary Flames on November 11, 1981, in a trade for the Flyer's Mel Bridgman. Marsh had already appeared in 17 games for the Flames at the time, but the Flyers had only completed the first 14 games of their schedule. When Marsh appeared in each of the Flyer's remaining 66 games, it gave him a total of 83 games played for the NHL 80-game regular season schedule. That broke the previous record for games played during a regular season, formerly held by Flyer winger Ross Lonsberry. He had played 50 games with the Los Angeles Kings during the 1971-72 season when he was traded along with three other players to the Flyers, who at the time had played four fewer games than the Kings. When Lonsberry played in each of the Flyers' remaining 32 games, he finished the year with 82 games played in the 78-game schedule played in the NHL in 1971-72.

5 The six original coaches named to guide the 1967 NHL expansion teams were: **Leonard "Red" Kelly** (Los Angeles), **Wren Blair** (Minnesota), **Keith Allen** (Philadelphia), **George "Red" Sullivan** (Pittsburgh), **Lynn Patrick** (St. Louis), and **Rudy Pilous** (Oakland). You might recall that it was **Bert Olmstead** who was behind the Oakland bench when they opened the season. That was because he replaced Pilous before the season started. So while Pilous was the first coach named for Oakland, he never actually coached them in a game.

6 The coaches of the six original NHL teams as the first expansion season (1967-68) opened were: **Harry Sinden** (Boston), **Billy Reay** (Chicago), **Sid Abel** (Detroit), **Toe Blake** (Montreal), **Punch Imlach** (Toronto), and **Emile Francis** (New York Rangers).

7 The fourteen cities which entered the NHL after 1967, their debut years, and their first coaches were:

Vancouver Canucks (1970),
  Hal Laycoe
Buffalo Sabres (1970),
  Punch Imlach
Atlanta Flames (1972),
  Bernie Geoffrion
New York Islanders (1972),
  Phil Goyette
Washington Capitals (1974),
  Jim Anderson
Kansas City Scouts (1974),
  Bep Guidolin
Colorado Rockies (1976),
  Johnny Wilson
Cleveland Barons (1976),
  Jack "Tex" Evans
Edmonton Oilers (1979),
  Glen Sather
Hartford Whalers (1979),
  Don Blackburn
Quebec Nordiques (1979),
  Jacques Demers
Winnipeg Jets (1979),
  Tom McVie
Calgary Flames (1980),
  Al MacNeil
New Jersey Devils (1982),
  Bill MacMillan

8 Late in the 1973-74 season Minnesota's Bill Goldsworthy became the first player to score 200 goals with an expansion team. He scored 48 goals for the North Stars that season, and was an original roster player with the club, which claimed him from the Boston Bruins in the NHL expansion draft.

9 The six current NHL cities previously represented in the NHL, and their earlier clubs, are:
Montreal, PQ—Montreal Wanderers (1917-18); **Montreal Maroons** (1924-38)
Quebec City, PQ—Quebec Bulldogs (1919-20)
Pittsburgh, PA—Pittsburgh Pirates (1925-30)
New York, NY—New York Americans (1925-42)
Philadelphia, PA—Philadelphia Quakers (1930-31)
St. Louis, MO—St. Louis Eagles (1934-35)

10 NHL President (1946-77) Clarence Sutherland Campbell, both a Rhodes Scholar and lawyer, served briefly at the end of WWII as a **war crimes prosecutor**.

11 The 1977-78 NHL season was a long one for veteran defenseman **Dennis O'Brien**. When it started, he was in his seventh season with the **Minnesota North Stars**, with whom he had played almost 500 games. The **Colorado Rockies** acquired him from Minnesota on waivers on December 2, 1977 but he spent just sixteen games with them before being traded to the **Cleveland Barons** on January 12, 1978, for another defenseman, Mike Christie. After twenty-three games with the Barons, his third NHL club of the season, O'Brien was on the move again. On March 10, 1978, the **Boston Bruins** claimed him on waivers to help them bolster their defense as they went into the play-offs. What makes O'Brien's odyssey ironic is that none of the first three teams he was with in 1977-78—Minnesota, Colorado and Cleveland—qualified for the play-offs that year. The Bruins, on the other hand, went to the Stanley Cup Finals before losing to the Montreal Canadiens.

12 **Anatoli Vladimirovich Tarasov**, considered by most to be the father of Soviet hockey, was elected to the Hockey Hall of Fame as a "Builder" in 1974.

13 While virtually all teams have used the traditional dark brown or black skates, three teams have experimented with colored ones. The **St. Louis Blues** tried a blue and gold boot to match their uniforms, and so did the **Oakland (California) Seals,** who tried both a green and gold and all-white skate. The short-lived WHA New York Golden Blades used an all snow-white boot.

14 Referee **Bill Chadwick**, who was elected to the Hall of Fame in 1964, turned to officiating because he **lost an eye**. In March, 1935, Chadwick was struck in the right eye during the warmup before an all-star game. He returned to play after the injury, which left him blind in that right eye only to be struck in the left eye the next season. He regained his vision in his left eye and, at the suggestion of the Rovers' manager, Tom Lockhart, turned to officiating and spent seventeen years as an NHL referee.

15 Signed by the Flyers as a free-agent rookie, **Al Hill** was called up from the AHL Springfield Indians to replace Harvey Bennett, who was injured a couple of nights earlier. Coach Fred Shero started the young winger on a line with Bob Clarke and Bob Kelly in his first NHL game on February 14, 1977, on a night when the St. Louis Blues were visiting the Spectrum in a nationally televised contest. Just thirty-six seconds into the game, Hill scored his first NHL goal. He was credited with his second eleven minutes later when he tipped in a shot by teammate Rick MacLeish. As the game wore on, Hill seemed to always be in the right place at the right time as he collected three assists to go along with his pair of goals. Those **five** points are the most ever scored by a player in his *first* NHL game. Unfortunately, a severe blizzard that night kept many people away, so this bit of NHL history was witnessed by just a few thousand brave hockey fans.

SUPER QUESTION ONE: "WHO IS THAT NHL'er FROM. . . BIG SPRING, TEXAS?"

Most of the men who have played in the National Hockey League over the years have been born in the Provinces of Canada, the Northern "hockey belt" of the United States (Minnesota, Michigan, and Massachusetts), and more recently, Sweden and Finland. But in recent years, players born in many other places have found their way to the NHL. In this first of our Super Questions, we have listed the birthplaces of twenty-six men who have played in the NHL since 1967 (although some started their NHL careers before expansion.) Each was born in a place which you would not expect to produce a professional hockey player, let alone one who would reach the world's premier professional circuit. Your challenge is to identify the NHL player who was born in each. After you have gone through the list and named as many as you are able, you may turn to the second part of this Super Question, in which a clue to the identity of each player is given to help you identify the ones you missed.

A. Big Spring, Texas
B. Cordenona, Italy
C. Sokolce, Czechoslovakia
D. Maaq, Taiwan (Nationalist China)
E. Washington, DC
F. Paraguay
G. Oakland, California
H. Caracas, Venezuela
I. Kuybichevki-Voftochany, Siberia (USSR)
J. Beirut, Lebanon
K. Birmingham, England
L. Frederick, Maryland
M. Zranjanin, Yugoslavia

N. Staten Island, NY
O. Cincinnati, Ohio
P. Ocala, Florida
Q. Weesp, Holland
R. Maracaibo, Venezuela
S. Yellowknife, Northwest Territory
T. Long Beach, California
U. Glasgow, Scotland
V. San Bernardino, Califonia
W. Emsdetten, Germany
X. Norfolk, Virginia
Y. Ellesmere, England
Z. Naliboki, Poland

THE CLUES

Now that you have gone through the list of unusual birthplaces, here is an additional clue to the identity of each mystery player.

A. A Denver University defenseman who played in the NHL with California, Cleveland, and Colorado.

B. A left wing with Detroit and Pittsburgh, his middle name is Flavio.

C. In 22 NHL seasons, all with one club, this three-time Art Ross Trophy-winner scored a career total of 541 regular-season goals.

D. This Norris Trophy-winner has also played in the WHA and on a Stanley Cup winner.
E. The son of.the president of a major international airline, this blueliner helped one of his NHL clubs to several Stanley Cup championships.
F. A not-so-gentle giant, this Calder Memorial Trophy-winner has toiled in three NHL cities.
G. A defenseman from the Oshawa Generals, he has seen NHL service with Washington and Quebec.
H. Raised in Erie, PA, he has played in the largest cities on each US coast, as well as on a Canadian-based Cup champion.
I. He scored a goal at Madison Square Garden in his first NHL game.
J. A player with Detroit and Vancouver, he appeared in 47 NHL games in two seasons.
K. Once a part of one of the biggest trades in NHL history early in his career. He was a 50-goal scorer with the Boston Bruins before ending his NHL career with the New York Rangers.
L. This 6'2" winger has NHL experience (Hartford, Montreal) but played first in the WHA.
M. His NHL career has taken him to six teams and seen him score over 300 goals.
N. While never a big scorer, his intensity has always made him a fan favorite while playing for his hometown team.
O. A tough left-winger with both Vancouver and Chicago, he was a second-round pick in 1978.
P. This defenseman was raised on Long Island (NY) and has scored an AHL Calder Cup championship-winning goal.
Q. A veteran defenseman with both Atlanta and St. Louis, he also played for the Jersey Devils in the Eastern Hockey League.
R. This player moved directly from the 1980 Winter Olympics to the Winnipeg Jets.
S. Once a first-round draft pick from the Medicine Hat Tigers, he played center for the Chicago Black Hawks.
T. A defenseman, he was a first-round pick in the 1980 draft.
U. A Boston Bruin right wing, he also played in the WHA and scored 50 goals in a single season in the AHL.
V. This Californian played junior hockey with the OHA Kitchener Rangers in the early 1970's before joining the Minnesota North Stars' blueline corps.
W. After a brief five-game minor league career with the AHL Buffalo Bisons, this checking center spent all of his thirteen-year NHL career with a single team.
X. The Buffalo Sabres signed this defenseman as a free agent in 1979 after he played college hockey with Northeastern University in Boston.
Y. The Montreal Canadiens drafted this right wing from the Ottawa 67's in the first round of the 1976 draft, but he has played his entire NHL career with the Pittsburgh Penguins.
Z. After playing defense for four NHL clubs during his career, he spent the last third of his twenty-year active career playing in Southern California.

MYSTERY PLAYER B

THE ANSWERS

A. **Mike Christie** (California, Cleveland, Colorado)
B. **Nelson Debenedet** (Detroit, Pittsburgh)
C. **Stan Mikita** (Chicago)
D. **Rod Langway** (Montreal, Washington)
E. **Bill Nyrop** (Montreal, Minnesota)
F. **Willi Plett** (Atlanta/Calgary, Minnesota)
G. **Lee Norwood** (Quebec, Washington)
H. **Rick Chartraw** (Montreal, Los Angeles, New York Rangers)
I. **Viktor Nechaev** (Los Angeles)
J. **Ed Hatoum** (Detroit, Vancouver)
K. **Ken Hodge** (Chicago, Boston, New York Rangers)
L. **Jeff Brubaker** (Hartford, Montreal)
M. **Ivan Boldirev** (Boston, California, Chicago, Atlanta, Vancouver, Detroit)
N. **Nick Fotiu** (New York Rangers, Hartford)
O. **Curt Fraser** (Vancouver, Chicago)
P. **Valmore James** (Buffalo)
Q. **Ed Kea** (Atlanta, St. Louis)
R. **Don Spring** (Winnipeg)
S. **Greg Vaydik** (Chicago)
T. **Rik Wilson** (St. Louis)
U. **Gordie Clark** (Boston)
V. **Chris Ahrens** (Minnesota)
W. **Walt Tkaczuk** (New York Rangers)
X. **Jim Walsh** (Buffalo)
Y. **Peter Lee** (Pittsburgh)
Z. **John Miszuk** (Detroit, Chicago, Philadelphia, Minnesota)

MYSTERY PLAYER C

PART II

"ALL IN THE FAMILY"...
HOCKEY'S FATHERS, SONS
& BROTHERS

Perhaps more than any other sport, hockey seems to be a "family" game. While it is relatively rare in most sports for more than one member of a family to make a name for himself in a particular sport, it is not at all uncommon in hockey. The questions we pose on the following few pages all "relate" to hockey-playing (or coaching) relations. While there are no "Bunkers" among them, they have nonetheless kept it "All In The Family."

1 Our first challenge to you is to name as many sets of professional hockey-playing brothers as you can. Our only restriction is that each must have played all or part of his career after 1967, and at least one member of each set of brothers had to have played in the NHL. (Just to give you a guideline, we'll tell you that we have come up with 106 sets representing 231 players.)

2 In the past few years, a single NHL team has had not just one but two players who were either a son or a nephew of a former NFL quarterback. What was the hockey team, who were the two players, and who were the two ex-NFL field generals they were related to?

3 Twice in recent years a player has been on an NHL team coached by his older brother. Who were these two coach/player brother duos, and what were their NHL clubs?

4 While brothers have frequently faced each other as opponents on the ice as players, just twice in NHL history have they coached against each other as NHL head coaches. Who were these two opposing coach/brother pairs, and what NHL clubs were they directing at the time?

5 In recent years one NHL team has had a pair of brothers who served the club as its head and assistant coaches. Who are they and what team did they coach together?

6 The city of Kirkland Lake, Ontario, has sent two sets of brothers to the NHL. All defensemen, they played a combined total of 47 seasons in the

league (as well as many more in the minors), and appeared in over 3,000 NHL games overall. Who were these veteran NHL blueliners, and what unusual (if unofficial) league record does one of them hold?

7 While brothers sometimes play together on the same team, only twice in NHL history have three brothers played together on the same *line*. Who were these two trios and what were their teams?

8 The rarest of hockey-playing relations seem to be goaltenders, but the NHL has had both a father-and-son duo and a pair of brothers that were all netminders. Who are these four goalies, what were their respective teams, and what virtually unbreakable record, set in 1941, does one of them hold?

9 The 1982-83 season saw six members of one family, all brothers, appear in NHL uniforms in the same campaign for the first time. Who were they, what were their teams, and how many total regular season and play-off games did these six brothers appear in during the 1982-83 season?

10 While many families have made contributions to hockey over the years, there is little doubt that one stands above them all. For three generations, members of this one family have played, coached, and managed in the NHL, and a single club has had one or more representatives of each of those three generations manage and/or coach it at one time or another. What is the name of this great hockey family, who have been its four most prominent members, and what team have all of them been associated with at one time or another over the past sixty years?

11 What family holds the single-season NHL "record" for total points?

12 What family holds the single-season NHL "record" for total goals?

13 What family holds the single-season NHL "record" for total assists?

14 What family holds the single-season NHL "record" for total penalty minutes?

15 In the history of the NHL, five pairs of brothers have combined career totals of at least: 1,800 games played; 700 goals; 875 assists; 1,600 points; and 1,700 penalty minutes (three of the five). Who are these five sets of NHL brothers, and which pair has the highest combined total in *each* of the five categories? (Totals are for regular season play only, not play-offs.)

"ALL IN THE FAMILY"...
ANSWERS

1 Here is our list of professional hockey-playing brothers. Of the following 106 sets of two or more brothers, at least one member of each set played in the NHL since 1967. (In fact in most cases, all of the brothers in each set has played all or part of his career in the league.) This has been one of the most interesting questions for us to do, because we ourselves didn't realize that there have been so many sets of brothers in recent years, and most of the professional hockey people we have asked to guess the number consistently underestimate it. We have done our best to find them all, and we extend our appologies to any we may have missed. As it is, our list of 106 represents a total of 231 players!!!

ALLISON, Dave & Mike
BABYCH, Wayne & David
BALON, Dave & Chick
BARBER, Bill, John & Dan
BARRETT, Fred & John
BENNETT, Curt, Harvey & Bill
BORDELEAU, J.P., Chris & Paulin
BROTEN, Aaron & Neal
BROWNSCHIDLE, Jack & Jeff
BUSNIUK, Mike & Ron
CALLANDER, Drew & Jock
CARLSON, Jack, Steve & Jeff
CHERRY, Don & Dick
CIRELLA, Joe & Carmine
CRAWFORD, Marc & Bob
CROWDER, Bruce & Keith
CULLEN, Barry, Ray & Brian
DINEEN, Gord, Peter, Kevin &
   & Shawn
DRYDEN, Ken & Dave
DUGUAY, Ron & Rick
EAVES, Mike & Murray
ESPOSITO, Phil & Tony
FERGUS, Tom & Dan
FLOCKHART, Rob & Ron
GARDNER, Paul & Dave
GASSOFF, Bob, Brad & Ken
GOULD, Larry & John
HAMEL, Jean & Gilles
HEXTALL, Bryan & Dennis
HOEKSTRA, Ed & Cecil

HICKE, Bill & Ernie
HICKEY, Pat & Greg
HICKS, Doug & Glenn
HILLMAN, Larry & Wayne
HOLT, Randy & Greg
HOWE, Mark & Marty
HULL, Bobby & Dennis
HUNTER, Dave, Dale & Mark
KANNEGEISER, Sheldon
   & Gordon
KITCHEN, Mike & Bill
KENNEDY, Forbes & Jamie
KLEINENDORST, Scot & Kurt
LAFOREST, Bob & Mark
LAMBERT, Lane & Ross
LARMER, Steve & Jeff
LEFLEY, Bryan & Chuck
MacLEISH, Rick & Dale
MacMILLAN, Billy & Bob
MAHOVLICH, Frank & Peter
MAKI, Chico & Wayne
MALONE, Greg & Jim
MALONEY, Don & Dave
MANERY, Kris & Randy
McANEELY, Ted & Bob
McCREARY, Bill & Keith
McKEGNEY, Tony, Mike & Ian
MELOCHE, Gilles & Denis
MESSIER, Paul & Mark
MOKOSAK, Carl & John
MOLLER, Randy & Mike

MULLEN, Joe & Brian
MULVEY, Paul & Grant
MURDOCH, Bob & Don
O'SHEA, Kevin & Danny
PAIEMENT, Rosaire & Wilf
PATEY, Larry & Doug
PATRICK, Craig & Glenn
PINDER, Gerry, Tom & Herb
PLUMB, Rob & Ron
PLAGER, Barclay, Bob & Bill
PLAYFAIR, Larry & Jim
POPEIL, Poul & Jan
POTVIN, Jean & Dennis
PRATT, Kelly & Tracy
PRONOVOST, Marcel & Jean
REDMOND, Mickey & Dick
RICHARD, Maurice & Henri
RISSLING, Gary & Kelly
ROBERTS, Doug & Gordie
ROBERTSON, Torrie & Gordie
ROBINSON, Larry & Moe
SAUVE, Bob & J.F.
SCHMAUTZ, Bobby & Cliff
SCHOCK, Ron & Danny

SCHULTZ, Dave & Ray
SEILING, Rod, Don & Ric
SHMYR, Paul & John
SHEEHY, Tim & Neil
SOBCHUK, Gene & Dennis
SITTLER, Darryl & Gary
SMITH, Gordie & Billy
STANFIELD, Fred, Jack & Jim
STASTNY, Marian, Peter & Anton
STANKIEWICZ, Myron & Ed
SUNDSTROM, Patrick & Peter
SUTTER, Brian, Darryl,
    Duane, Brent, Ron & Rich
TREMBLAY, J.C. & Ray
TROTTIER, Bryan, Rocky & Monty
VAIVE, Rick & Jeff
WALTON, Mike & Robbie
WATSON, Joe & Jimmy
WILLIAMS, Frederick R. & Gordie
WILLIAMS, Warren & Tommy
WILSON, Murray & Doug
WILSON, Behn & Bart
YAREMCHUK, Gary & Ken

2 Boston Bruin defenseman **Mike O'Connell** is the son of former Cleveland Browns quarterback **Tommy O'Connell**. Right wing **Tom Songin**, a former Bruin, also has NFL blood in his background as the nephew of former New England Patriots' QB **"Butch" Songin**.

3 As GM/coach of the Colorado Rockies and the same club when it moved East to become the New Jersey Devils, **Billy MacMillan** both traded for and coached his younger brother, **Bob**. Veteran defenseman Terry Murray finished his playing career with the Washington Capitals in 1981-82. Just fifteen games into that campaign, Gary Green was replaced behind the Caps bench by **Bryan Murray**, Terry's older brother, who was promoted from the Capitals' AHL development club, the Hershey Bears.

4 **Lynn** and **Muzz Patrick** coached against each other during parts of the 1953-54 and 1954-55 seasons, when Lynn was coach of the **Boston Bruins** and brother Muzz was behind the bench of the **New York Rangers**. The only other time that brothers faced each other from behind the bench came on January 20, 1977, at Olympia Stadium in Detroit when the visiting **Colorado Rockies**, coached by veteran NHL mentor **Johnny Wilson**, defeated the **Detroit Red Wings**, 3-1, who were then being guided by his brother, **Larry Wilson**. (In a touch of added irony, the teams' two trainers were also named Wilson, Lefty with Detroit, Toby for Colorado—but they were not related.)

5 In 1982, defenseman **Terry Murray** retired as a player and joined his brother, **Bryan**, to become his assistant coach with the **Washington Capitals**. Bryan had become head coach of the Caps in mid-November, 1981, and coached brother Terry until he retired to join him as a coach.

6 **Larry and Wayne Hillman** and **Barclay, Bob, and Bill Plager** all grew up together in Kirkland Lake, Ontario, in the 1940's and 50's and went on to long NHL careers. All three Plager brothers played together with the St. Louis Blues in the late 1960's and early 1970's, while the Hillmans were teammates in NHL play only with the Philadelphia Flyers (1969-71). Larry Hillman has the distinction of belonging to more NHL clubs—eleven—than any other player in history. Starting with Detroit in 1954, he also played for Boston, Toronto, Minnesota, Montreal, Philadelphia, Los Angeles, and Buffalo. In addition, his contract was owned by three other NHL clubs, Chicago, New York Rangers, and Pittsburgh, for whom he never played. In the minor leagues he played for Edmonton (WHL), Buffalo, Springfield, Providence, and Rochester (all AHL) and finished his playing career with three seasons in the WHA with Cleveland and Winnipeg before he hung up his skates for the last time in 1976. In a twenty-two-year pro playing career, Larry Hillman played for or belonged to a total of *eighteen* teams, and coincidently many of those won championships while he was a member of them. He may have been traded often, but he was a winner everywhere he went.

7 The NHL's first all-brother line was made up of **Reggie, Max, and Doug Bentley**, who played together briefly as a unit for the **Chicago Black Hawks** during the 1942-43 season. In 1981, Czech brothers **Peter, Anton, and Marian Stastny** were reunited by the Quebec Nordiques. Together they contributed a total of 304 points (120 goals, 184 assists) during regular season and play-off action in 1982-83.

8 **Sam LoPresti** set an NHL record on March 4, 1941, when as a goalie for the Chicago Black Hawks he stopped a record 80 of 83 shots by the Boston Bruins in a game played at Boston Garden. Despite his titanic effort, he lost the game, 3-2. His son, **Pete**, followed him to the NHL, where he played goal for six seasons between 1974 and 1981. Of his 177 career NHL games, all but two came with the Minnesota North Stars. His other two appearances were with the Edmonton Oilers.

The NHL's only brother goaltending duo consisted of **Dave and Ken Dryden**. Older brother Dave (9 NHL seasons) appeared in a total of 206 NHL games with the New York Rangers, Chicago Black Hawks, Buffalo Sabres, and Edmonton Oilers. He also played another 179 WHA games with Chicago and Edmonton. Younger brother Ken played his entire NHL career with just one club, the Montreal Canadiens. In 397 regular season games for the Habs over eight seasons (1971-73 and 1974-79) Ken compiled a 2.24 goals-against average (46 shut-outs). He also backstopped the Canadiens to six Stanley Cup championships with a 2.40 post-season average in 112 contests (10 shut-outs) before retiring in 1979. He was elected to the Hockey Hall of Fame in 1983 at age 35, and is currently practicing law in Canada.

9 The **Sutter brothers** combined for a total of 385 NHL games in 1982-83. **Brian** (St. Louis) and **Darryl** (Chicago) both also served as captains of their teams. **Duane** and **Brent** (New York Islanders) both helped their club to a fourth Stanley Cup, and twins **Ron** (Philadelphia) and **Rich** (Pittsburgh) were both recalled briefly from the WHL Lethbridge Broncos. On October 23, 1983, Rich was traded to the Flyers, and six days later he and Ron faced brothers Duane and Brent of the Isles—the first time in NHL history that four brothers appeared in the *same* game.

10 The **Patrick** family has been associated with the **New York Rangers** almost without interruption since the team was established in 1926. **Lester Patrick** played for, coached, or managed the team from 1926 to 1946. His sons, *Lynn* and **"Muzz"** both played for and later coached the team. An All-Star winger, Lynn coached the team from 1948 to 1950 before going to coach the Boston Bruins and later coach and manage the St. Louis Blues. A long-time Ranger defenseman, "Muzz" was GM and/or coach of the Rangers from 1955 to 1964. There was then a sixteen-season hiatus until Lynn's son, **Craig**, became the Rangers' Director of Operations in 1980. An eight-year NHL player with California, St. Louis, Kansas City, and Washington, Craig served as captain of the U.S. National Team in the 1979 world championships in Moscow. The following year he was manager and assistant coach of the 1980 Gold Medal-winning U.S. Olympic team.

Craig coached the Rangers for much of the 1980-81 season after Fred Shero left the team. He was named Vice President and General Manager of the team before the start of the 1981-82 season, a position which both his uncle and grandfather had held before him.

The Rangers play within the **Patrick Division** in the NHL, which was named for his grandfather, Lester, as was the **Lester Patrick Trophy**, an NHL award presented for ". . . outstanding service to hockey in the United States." He also gave his name to the Lester Patrick Cup which was awarded to the play-off champions of the Western Hockey League until that professional circuit ceased operations in 1974.

11 **Peter, Anton, and Marian Stastny**, all of the **Quebec Nordiques**, hold the single-season family "record" for total points in the NHL with 290 (108 goals, 182 assists) during regular season play in 1982-83.

12 **Brian, Darryl, Duane, Brent, Ron, and Rich Sutter** set the "record"

for total goals by a family with 112, also during the 1982-83 regular season.

13 The Stastnys'total of 182 assists in 1982-83 gives them that family mark.

14 The Sutter sextet compiled a total of 562 penalty minutes in 1982-83. It should be noted that with both families expected to be active in the NHL for quite a few more years, these records will probably be broken a number of times during the 1980s.

15 Here are the five sets of NHL brothers that have combined as pairs for at least 1,800 games played, 700 goals scored, 875 assists, 1,600 points, and (three of the five) 1,700 penalty minutes:

PLAYERS/BROTHERS (NHL SEASONS)

	GP	G	A	PTS	PIM
Maurice Richard (18) Montreal	978	544	421	965	1,285
Henri Richard (20) Montreal	1,256	358	688	1,046	928
TOTALS	2,234	902	1,109	2,011	2,213
Bobby Hull (16) Chi., Winn., Htfd.	1,063	610	560	1,170	640
Dennis Hull (14) Chicago, Detroit	959	303	351	654	261
TOTALS	2,022	913	911	1,824	901
Frank Mahovlich (17) Tor., Det., Mtl.	1,181	533	570	1,103	1,056
Peter Mahovlich (16) Det., Mtl., Pitt.	884	288	485	773	916
TOTALS	2,065	821	1,055	1,876	1,972

Those first three pair of great high-scoring NHL brothers were probably fairly easy for you, but the other two are a little more tricky. If you get these two pairs, you are a top Hockey Trivia expert!!

PLAYER/BROTHERS (NHL SEASONS)

	GP	G	A	PTS	PIM
Gordie Howe (26) Detroit, Hartford	1,767	801	1,049	1,850	1,685
Vic Howe (3) New York Rangers	33	3	4	7	34
TOTALS	1,800	804	1,053	1,857	1,719
Phil Esposito (18) Chi., Bost., NYR	1,282	717	873	1,590	910
Tony Esposito (15*) Mtl., Chicago	868*	0*	15*	15*	31*
TOTALS	2,150*	717*	888*	1,605*	941*

[*Through 1982-83 season]

Bobby and Dennis Hull lead the pack in total combined career Goals with 913. Maurice and Henri Richard are tops in the other four catagories with the most combined career Games Played (2,234), Assists (1,109), Points (2,213), and Penalty Minutes (2,213).

SUPER QUESTION TWO: GREAT FORWARD LINES . . . WHEN THREE IS MORE THAN ONE

O ver the course of a season, many "lines" are put together as each team looks for the best blend of talent among their forwards to make them a winner. Some lines may last no longer than a game, or just a few shifts. Others survive for a few weeks, or perhaps as long as a whole season. But occasionally a combination is formed that transcends the high level of skill of "regular" NHL play to become something special and lasting. There have been many great lines over the history of the NHL that have spent many seasons playing as a unit. In no other sport does a group of individual players work more as one than in hockey. And there is perhaps no greater artistry in sport than the magic these great lines weave on the ice— trio—of immensely talented and skilled athletes performing their wizardry with grace and speed.

We have listed below the numbers of thirty-three NHL players who have played on eleven of the greatest lines in the league since expansion in 1967. Your task is to group them into the eleven lines, identify the players, and name the team each trio played for.

Left Wings: 7, 7, 9, 9, 10, 11, 11, 12, 18, 21, 22
Centers: 7, 7, 11, 16, 16, 16, 19, 19, 25, 26, 27
Right Wings: 7, 7, 8, 8, 8, 10, 14, 18, 20, 22, 27

This Super Question is not expected to be easy, but with a little thought and work, the knowledgeable hockey observer should be able to figure out most of them. After you have identified as many as you can just from the numbers above you may turn to the next page for the first of two clues about the identity of the lines.

THE FIRST CLUE

Here is the first of two clues to help you identify these eleven great forward lines. We have grouped the thirty-three players numerically into their line combinations. The numbers of the players on each line are listed from lowest to highest, which does not necessarily coincide with their positions of left wing, center, and right wing.

Line A:	7 — 8 — 9	Line:	8 — 16 — 21
Line B:	7 — 8 — 10	Line H:	9 — 19 — 22
Line C:	7 — 11 — 14	Line I:	10 — 22 — 25
Line D:	7 — 11 — 19	Line J:	11 — 16 — 18
Line E:	7 — 12 — 27	Line K:	18 — 20 — 26
Line F:	7 — 16 — 27		

THE SECOND CLUE

Now that you have had a chance to work on the lines with the player numbers grouped together correctly, we will now give you a second clue to help you identify any which may still be puzzling you.

A. Each of the three players on this great line started his NHL career with a club *other* than the one with which he became famous as a member of this trio. These three men combined for a total of 1,717 goals in their careers.
B. Known as the "MPH Line," this trio was famous not so much for their speed as for their smoothness and fine passing.
C. One of the three French-Canadian players on this line was the first player ever drafted by the club for which this trio played together, and he remained a member of the team after all his other original-roster teammates were gone.
D. Two of these three linemates grew up together in hockey and were teammates with four other clubs before playing together in the NHL for almost a decade.
E. All three members of this line were eventually traded to other clubs where they played with distinction.
F. As the "LCB Line" they helped their club to a Stanley Cup championship in their first season as NHL teammates. Two members of the trio had been record-setting linemates in junior hockey years earlier.
G. Two members of this trio broke into the NHL with Montreal and the third played with Boston before they became a high-scoring unit with an expansion team.
H. Two of these linemates were their club's first two selections in the 1974 draft, while the third was taken in the first round of the draft in 1977.
I. This line was a key to four consecutive Stanley Cup championships.
J. One winger on this line came to his club as a minor league free agent while the other was a 15th-round draft pick (210th overall).
K. These three linemates have known each other *all* their lives.

MYSTERY PLAYER D

THE ANSWERS

Here are the names (and numbers) of the thirty-three players who made up our eleven great post-expansion NHL lines (left wing/center/right wing) and the clubs with which they played.

A. **Johnny Bucyk** (9) - **Phil Esposito** (7) - **Ken Hodge** (8) [Boston Bruins]

B. **Dennis Hull** (10) - **Pit Martin** (7) - **Jim Pappin** (8) [Chicago Black Hawks]

C. **Rick Martin** (7) - **Gil Perreault** (11) - **Rene Robert** (14) [Buffalo Sabres]

D. **Vic Hadfield** (11) - **Jean Ratelle** (19) - **Rod Gilbert** (7) [New York Rangers]

E. **Errol Thompson** (12) - **Darryl Sittler** (27) - **Lanny McDonald** (7) [Toronto Maple Leafs]

F. **Bill Barber** (7) - **Bob Clarke** (16) - **Reggie Leach** (27) [Philadelphia Flyers]

G. **Danny Grant** (21) - **Jude Drouin** (16) - **Bill Goldsworthy** (8) [Minnesota North Stars]

H. **Clark Gillies** (9) - **Bryan Trottier** (19) - **Mike Bossy** (22) [New York Islanders]

I. **Steve Shutt** (22) - **Jacques Lemaire** (25) - **Guy Lafleur** (10) [Montreal Canadians]

J. **Charlie Simmer** (11) - **Marcel Dionne** (16) - **Dave Taylor** (18) [Los Angeles Kings]

K. **Anton Stastny** (20) - **Peter Stastny** (26) - **Marian Stastny** (18) [Quebec Nordiques]

PART III

OF PENALTIES, SHOTS & PENALTY SHOTS . . . NHL RULES

Most hockey fans are familiar with the basic rules of the game. The concepts of minor and major penalties, face-offs, icings, goal scoring, etc., are all pretty clear. But for the officials in charge of each game—referee, linesmen, goal judges, scorers, timekeepers, and other off-ice officials—the understanding, interpretation, and application of the 85 NHL Rules must be both complete and correct. Those rules take approximately 17,500 words to spell out, and must be applied quickly in thousands of different situations under the scrutiny of an arena-full of emotional, partisan fans. And they must be applied fairly and impartially to men playing an intense physical game. It is often said, and is in many ways true, that the only sane people in the building during a hockey game are the officials.

On the following pages you will find a number of hypothetical, but quite possible, game situations which call for a ruling by an official. Read the *whole* set of conditions existing in each situation and then consider the question carefully and decide what you would call if you were the referee. Be careful, as some of the conditions may not be relevant, or may be in some way misleading if you do not consider them in the light of an *entire* set of circumstances. After you have made your "call," turn to the answer section of this question for a full explanation of what the correct call is and why.

NOTE: To make each question clearer, in most cases we have given names to players and teams in our questions. In all cases, your rulings should be based on NHL RULES even if we have not used the names of NHL teams.

1 Defenseman "Farmer" Gruppioni of the Springfield Braves has been assessed a major penalty by you for spearing and a minor penalty for unsportsmanlike conduct at 7:24 of the third period. Assuming there were no other penalties being served at the time of the major-minor to Gruppioni, and no others are called on either Springfield or its opposition, the Jamaica Hawks, over the next ten minutes of play, at what time would Gruppioni be allowed out of the penalty box if the Hawks scored goals at 9:27, 12:23, 13:17, and 14:23?

2 Los Angeles Kings center Dan Bonar ices the puck, and linemate Dave Taylor and New Jersey Devils defenseman Bob Hoffmeyer chase it down the ice. The puck hits the boards behind Devils goalie Chico Resch and deflects out in front of the goal just as the two players reach it. As they arrive, Hoffmeyer reaches around Taylor and touches the puck first, but in doing so knocks it into his own goal and the goal judge turns on the red light. Do you rule that a goal has been scored?

3 With the Philadelphia Firebirds shorthanded, Firebird left-winger Randy Osburn clears the puck from his defensive zone and goes to the bench for a line change. Bim McFall of the Mohawk Valley Comets picks up the puck behind his own net and starts to move back up the ice. As he rounds the net he is checked immediately by the Firebirds' Peter Cahill and he passes the puck across the ice in front of his net to a Comets teammate. In doing so it hits the skate of the Comets' goalie and is deflected into the net. Do you allow a goal, and if so, to whom is it credited?

4 In the final minute of a game which the Cleveland Barons lead, 7-5, the Colorado rockies pull their goalie for an extra attacker. After the substitution has been made, Charlie Simmer of the Barons picks up the puck right in front of the Rockies' bench. As he does so, the Colorado trainer reaches over the boards and grabs Simmer's jersey. What call do you make, if any?

5 Goalie Bob Froese of the Saginaw Gears makes a glove save on a shot from the left point. With no teammates close by to drop the puck to, he sees fellow Gear Gordie Brooks breaking up the boards near the blueline and throws the puck to him. Brooks takes it on the fly just as he crosses into the neutral zone and heads up the ice. Do you stop play for any reason?

6 During play, Charlestown Chiefs goalie Denis Lemieux breaks his stick but continues to play with part of it until a stoppage in play when he skates to the bench to get a new one. Do you call a penalty on Lemeiux for playing with a broken stick?

7 The Montana Magic lead the Tulsa Oilers, 3-1, with forty seconds to go in the game. Montana has one man in the penalty box and Tulsa two, and none of the penalties are scheduled to expire before the end of regulation play. The Oilers pull their goalie on the fly but deliberately substitute *two* men for him so they will have five skaters (no goalie) on the ice, to Montana's four skaters and a goalie. Do you assess a bench minor on Tulsa for illegal substitution (Too Many Men on the Ice), or make any other call?

8 In the second period of a game between the Philadelphia Flyers and Montreal Canadiens, the Flyers are a man short when you raise your arm to indicate a delayed penalty on the Canadiens. With the Flyers retaining possession of the puck, their goalie, Pelle "Gump" Lindbergh, skates to the bench for an extra attacker. Just as he crosses center ice and arrives at the bench, but *before* he is substituted for, the puck comes to Lindbergh and he passes it on to a teammate. What, if anything, do you do at that instant?

9 You have awarded a penalty shot to New York Rovers' right wing Murdo McKay, who was pulled down on a break away by Swatso Bregoli of the Springfield Braves. You place the puck at center ice, inform Springfield goalie Earl Moren that he is to remain in his crease until the shot has begun, and send the players on the ice from both teams to the boards behind the red line. On your signal, McKay picks up the puck at center ice and, to the surprise of everybody in the building, skates back into his *own* defensive zone and circles behind the Rover net. He then starts to zig-zag back up the ice and as he passes through the neutral zone Springfield's Fritz Balboni charges past him on his way to complain to you that what McKay is doing is illegal. McKay hesitates then shoots just as he reaches the blueline. The puck sails directly over the net and rebounds off the glass, hitting Moren in the back, falling to the ice, and rolling into the net. The goal judge turns on the red light. What do you rule?

10 With thirty-six seconds left in the game, the Portland Buckaroos are leading the Seattle Totems, 1-0. Seattle's Larry McNab takes a shot on Portland goalie Marv Edwards which he stops—but in the process he loses his catching glove and it is inadvertantly kicked aside by a teammate. Fearing both possible injury and losing his shut-out, Edwards slides his back under the crossbar and deliberately dislodges the net to get a stoppage of play. You blow the whistle. Do you do anything else?

And now for a few strange calls that actually happened . . .

11 On November 19, 1981, the Hershey Bears were playing the Rochester Americans in an AHL contest at the Rochester War Memorial. At 13:16 of the third period the game was tied, 2-2, when referee Bob Hall awarded Rochester's Bob Mongrain a penalty shot when he was pulled down on a break away while the Americans were on a power play. Mongrain had been using an illegal stick up to that point in the game which had been noted by Hershey's Chris Valentine, who had reported his observation to Bears' coach Gary Inness. When Mongrain was awarded the penalty shot, he skated to the bench and exchanged his suspect stick for one he was sure was legal—an act of which most, but apparently not all, of his teammates were aware. Mongrain then took the penalty shot on Hershey goalie Al Jensen and scored.

Mongrain returned to the Rochester bench to celebrate his goal while the Bears immediately challenged his stick claiming the curve of its blade was greater than the regulation maximum of one-half inch. Referee Hall skated to the Americans' bench and asked Mongrain for his stick but before he could surrender it, a teammate who did not realize he had changed sticks before taking the shot stepped on the blade with his skate and broke it. What did referee Hall rule under the circumstances?

12 On November 12, 1981, veteran minor league right winger Randy MacGregor was called up from the Binghamton Whalers to play two games with the NHL Hartford Whalers. His first NHL action came against the Philadelphia Flyers at the Spectrum in Philadelphia. Early in the third period, with the Flyers leading, 3-1, MacGregor took a pass from Warren Miller at the Flyer blueline and started toward the Philadelphia net. As he did so he was pulled down by defenseman Frank Bathe and ended up in a sitting position on top of the puck sliding backwards. His and Bathe's momentum carried both of them, and the puck, into the Flyer net. Did referee Bruce Hood award MacGregor a goal?

13 On January 15, 1983, the New Jersey Devils visited the Hartford Whalers for the only time during the 1982-83 season. Because of a severe blizzard, only one of the three on-ice officials had arrived before the game. Was he required to officiate the game by himself, and if not, where could he go for help?

14 On November 28, 1979, the Colorado Rockies were beating the New York Islanders by a couple of goals as the game wound down to its final minutes at McNichols Arena in Denver, CO. With Islander goalie Billy Smith pulled for an extra man, Colorado right wing Randy Pierce scored an insurance goal into the empty New York net. He was so pleased with himself that he retrieved the puck personally, kissed it, and tossed it over the glass to the cheering Rockies fans. How did the referee react to this display of enthusiasm?

NHL RULES . . . ANSWERS

1 The penalized Springfield player, Gruppioni, would be released at 13:17. Under Rule 27(c), when a player receives both a major and minor penalty at the same time (and they are not coincident with similar penalties to a player from the other team), the major penalty is served first and then the minor. Rule 28(a) provides that a major penalty does not terminate when a goal is scored therefore; Gruppioni would remain in the box when the Hawks scored at 9:27 and 12:23. The final two minutes of the seven called against him, however, are for the minor penalty for unsportsmanlike conduct and are served after the major penalty has expired. Rule 27(a) permits a penalized player to return to the ice when a goal is scored if he is serving a minor penalty, which was the case when Jamaica scored at 13:17.

2 Your ruling is **"No Goal."** Even though the puck was deflected into the net by a defending player, at the instant he touched it play had in fact stopped for an icing under Rule 61 **(a-3).** If the puck had first been touched by the attacking player, Taylor (assuming that he was not offside and there was no foul pending against his team), and had then been deflected into the net by the defender, it would have been a legal goal [Rule **55(a)**]. When Hoffmeyer touched it first for the Devils, it was returned to the Kings' zone and faced-off.

3 You rule a legal **goal** has been scored and the official scorer awards it to **Osburn,** who was sitting on the bench when the puck entered the net, as an "unassisted goal" under Rule **55(b).** That rule provides for the awarding of a goal if the puck is deflected into the net by a defending player (the Comet goalie) and requires that credit be given to the last attacking player to touch the puck for an unassisted goal.

4 You award an **automatic goal** to the Barons under Rule **62(f).** Any interference from the bench of a team that has pulled its goalie (Colorado) with either the puck or an opposing player results in an automatic goal for the non-offending team. If the interference had occurred while the Colorado goalie was still on the ice, the penalty would be a two-minute minor against the offending Rockie player or on the bench if a non-player (manager, coach, trainer) had caused the interference [Rule **62(b)**].

5 You **stop** play immediately and call a **minor penalty** on Froese, the Saginaw goalie. Rule **57(b)** prohibits a goalkeeper from advancing the puck towards the opponent's goal with his hands. The only way a goalie can make a forward pass is with his stick.

6 Lemieux does **not** get a **penalty** for playing with a broken stick, but he **does** get one for going to the bench for a new one. Rule **46(b)** provides that a goalkeeper, and only goalkeepers, may continue to play with either a broken stick or a new stick delivered (but not thrown) to him by a teammate **[46(c)].** If the goalie goes to the bench at any time (other than for a substitution) to get a new stick, he is assessed a minor penalty under Rule **46(d).** Any player (including the goalkeeper) who receives a stick which has been thrown to him either from his bench or a teammate on the ice receives a minor penalty under Rule 46(c).

7 You award the Montana Magic a **penalty shot** under Rule **18(b).** That rule provides for a penalty shot when a team (Tulsa) deliberately makes an illegal substitution when the bench minor penalty that would otherwise be called for (Too Many Men on the Ice) cannot be served *in its entirety* by reason of insufficient playing time remaining or penalties already imposed. Both conditions would be met in this case and a penalty shot would be awarded.

8 You immediately blow your whistle to **stop** play and give **concurrent**

minor penalties to both Flyers' goalie Lindbergh and the Canadien who was to be called for the delayed minor. The Flyers are *not* being penalized for "Too Many Men on the Ice" [Rule 18(a-2)], because the goalie had not yet been substituted for. The penalty on Lindbergh is for violation of Rule **32(i)** which prohibits a goalkeeper from participating in play *beyond* the center-ice red line, which Lindbergh had crossed to reach his bench before he played the puck. Lindbergh would return to his crease after you stopped play and a player on the ice at the time would have to serve his minor for him under Rule **32(a).** The Montreal player (unless it was their goalie) would also go to the box, but both the Flyer and Canadien players would be immediately substituted for under Rule **27(d)** because the concurrent minor penalties came when the two teams were at uneven strength. The two players serving the concurrent minors could not leave the penalty boxes until the first stoppage of play after the previous short-handed situation was over [Rule 28(c)].

9   You rule: a) **No goal,** and; b) McKay is entitled to *another* **penalty shot.** Under Rule **31(a),** the shot was complete the instant the puck crossed the plane of the goal line which happened when it flew over the net and hit the glass. But Springfield's Balboni was guilty of violation of Rule **31(f)** when he distracted McKay by skating past him to complain to you as the referee during the first shot. Not only was that illegal, his complaint also had no merit. Rule **31(a)** allows the shooter to: " . . . carry the puck in any part of the Neutral Zone or his own Defending Zone . . . " The rule *only* requires the puck to be kept in motion towards the opponent's goal after crossing the "Attacking Blue Line."

10   Seattle is awarded a **penalty shot** under Rule **50(d)** because Portland's goalie deliberately dislodged his own goal. Such an action normally calls for a minor penalty [Rule **50(c)**], unless such a penalty cannot be served *in its entirety* because of insufficient playing time remaining or penalties already imposed. Rule 50(c) also provides, however, for a penalty shot to be awarded at any point in the game if a defending team displaces its net during a "break away."

11   Referee Hall correctly ruled both: a) **No Goal,** and; b) Mongrain should be assessed a **ten-minute misconduct penalty.** Rule **20(f)** provides for minor and misconduct penalties to be assessed against any player who fails to surrender a challenged stick in a condition in which it can be measured. Rule **20(e)** disallows any goal scored on a penalty shot with an illegal stick and vacates the minor penalty that would otherwise be called. Hall, therefore, disallowed the goal because failure to surrender the stick is prima facie evidence that it was illegal, and assessed a ten-minute misconduct (without the minor) for failure to surrender the stick after an otherwise successful penalty shot.

12   Hood awarded MacGregor his first, and only, NHL **goal.** Under Rule **55(b),** the goal was legal even though the puck was carried into the net

under MacGregor's body because *both* were put there by the actions of a defending player.

13 If two of the three officials had arrived by game time, they would have worked without additional help with one acting as linesman and the other as referee. But in this case only one official was on hand, so the provisions of Rule **36(k)** were applied to appoint **emergency officials** to replace assigned officials who could not work the game because of misadventure or sickness.

If qualified substitute officials cannot be found (as was the case that night), or cannot be agreed upon by the managers or coaches of the two clubs, then a player from each team is appointed to act as linesmen, and the official who made it to the game serves as the referee. In this case New Jersey's **Garry Howett** and Hartford's **Mickey Volcan** were selected; dressed in dark sweatsuits, they served as linesmen for the first period. Two additional NHL officials arrived in time for the second period and worked the rest of the game. (Neither Howatt nor Volcan were called upon to break up any fights.)

A similar situation occured on December 1, 1974, when a snowstorm prevented the referee and a linesman from getting to Philadelphia for a game between the Flyers and the Kansas City Scouts. With only veteran linesman **Matt Pavelich** on hand, the Spectrum's visiting team stickboys, **Mike Fore** and **Tom Capaccio** (both local amateur officials) were pressed into service for the first 8:17 of the game, until referee **Andy Van Hellemond** arrived and took over for Pavelich, who worked the rest of the game as solo linesman. Fore still works the visiting bench at the Spectrum.

In a case when **no** officials make it to the game and local ones cannot be located, the rule provides that one player from each team be assigned with the home player as referee and the visiting player as linesman.

14 Pierce was assessed a two-minute minor penalty for **Delay of the Game.** Under Rule **50(a),** a minor penalty is imposed on any player who deliberately throws or bats the puck outside of the playing surface at any time including during a stoppage of play.

SUPER QUESTION THREE: BIRDS, BEES & BEARS . . . HOCKEY TEAM LOGOS

E very hockey team is identified not only by a colorful uniform but also by a distinctive crest or logo. This crest almost always appears somewhere on each player's jersey and is defended with pride by its wearer. On the following pages you will find forty-five such crests or logos which have been adopted by professional or junior hockey teams in the United States and Canada. Many of the teams are still active, others are not; but all except one have played since 1966. Some logos have been used by more than one playing franchise, either in a different city and/or league. Some are just one of several that the team may have used over its life.

Our challenge to you is to identify a *specific* team that has used each logo. In order to do that you will have to refer to *both* the crest and the clue that goes with each (a list of players who have been a member of that specific team at some point in his career.) In order to make this Super Question a little more interesting, all but two of the logos have been *altered* in some way or another. But each retains enough of its distinctive shape for the experienced hockey-watcher to identify it.

Each logo appears in its original form in the answer section of this Super Question.

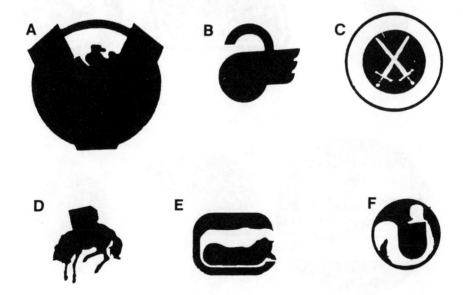

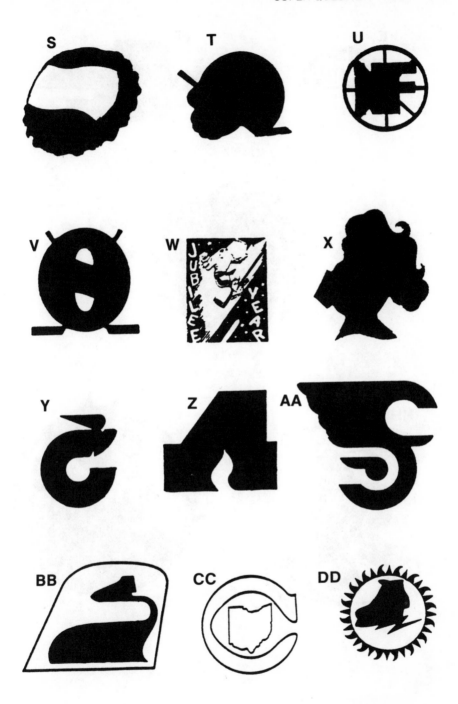

EE

FF

GG

HH

II

JJ

KK

LL

MM

NN

OO

PP

QQ

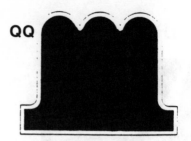

RR

SS

THE CLUES

Each of the following lists contains the names of players who have played for each mystery team at some point in each man's career.

A. Dwight Schofield, Larry Robinson, Yvon Lambert, Joe Hardy, Noel Price, Jeff Mars

B. Dave Schultz, Bob Currier, Simon Nolet, Bobby Taylor, Rene Drolet, Andre Lacroix

C. Rick Dudley, Billy Inglis, Ray McKay, Ron Busniuk, Terry Ball

D. Duane Sutter, Brian Sutter, Bryan Trottier, Les Crozier, Ron Sutter

E. Darryl Maggs, Pat Stapleton, Ralph Backstrom, Joe Hardy, Reg Fleming, Andre Gill

F. Gerry Pinder, Gary Jarrett, Gerry Cheevers, Rich Pumple, Skip Krake, Paul Shmyr

G. George Gardner, Richard Campeau, Colin Campbell, Bryan Campbell, Jim Cardiff

H. Reid Bailey, Al Hill, Rick Blight, Peter Dineen, Garry Unger

I. Marc Tardiff, Alton White, Jim Watson, Bart Crashley, George Gardner, J.P. LeBlanc

J. Chico Resch, Dennis Patterson, Bob Nystrom, Eddie Johnstone, Bobby Sheehan

K. Mark Howe, Jeff Woodyatt, Bernie Johnston, Glen Goldup, Mike Palmateer

L. Carl Brewer, Pat Hickey, Guy Trottier, Les Binkley, Wayne Carleton

M. Fred Shero, Dennis Patterson, Emile Francis, Bill Masterton, John Ferguson, Bob Berry

N. Mike Boland, Brian Conacher, Gavin Kirk, Ron Clime, Gilles Gratton

O. Tim Horton, Frank Mathers, Baz Bastien, Willie Marshall, Art Stratton

P. Danny Lawson, Butch Deadmarsh, Rick Jodzio, Bobby Leiter, Ron Chipperfield

Q. Rejean Lemelin, Sudsy Settlemyre, Bobby Collyard, Randy Osburn, Norm Barnes

R. Richie Hart, Peter Jack, Clay Hebenton, Willie O'Ree, Billy Goldthorpe, Bob Sauve

S. Gregg Pilling, Brad Park, Vic Hadfield, Ed Van Impe, Phil Maloney, Jerry Melnyk

T. Guido Tenisi, Greg Neeld, Mark Izzard, John Flesch, Gordie Laxton, Gary Carr

U. Bernie Parent, Bob Froese, Phil Myre, Doug Favell, Derek Sanderson

V. Paul Holmgren, Dave Keon, Mike Walton, Rick Smith, Ted Hampson, Len Lilyholm

W Clint Smith, Kilby MacDonald, Lude Wareing, Phil Hergesheimer, Eddie Bush

X. Darryl Sittler, Gordie Brooks, Randy Osburn, Denis Maruk, Reg Thomas

Y.   Michel Dion, Robbie Ftorek, Jamie Hislop, Paul Stewart, Mike Liut, Gordie Clark

Z.   Butch Deadmarsh, Noel Price, Pat Quinn, Rejean Lemelin, Phil Myre, Don Martineau

AA.   Ted McAneeley, Guy Bohmer, Rudy Tajcnar, Larry Hale, Kirk Fyffe, Don Dirk

BB   Wayne Gretzky, Gary Inness, Ed Mio, Blaine Stoughton, Kevin Morrison, Dave Inkpen

CC.   Glenn Patrick, Jim Pappin, Len Frig, Randy Holt, Denis Maruk, Charlie Simmer

DD.   Harry Howell, Andre Lacroix, Kevin Morrison, Wayne Rivers, Dean Boylan

EE.   Alton White, Jamie Kennedy, Claude Chartre, Wally Olds, Bobby Sheehan

FF.   B.J. MacDonald, Tim Tookey, Lee Norwood, Sylvain Cote, Andre Cote, Alain Cote

GG.   Merv Dubchak, Dan Bonar, Len Thornson, Robbie Laird, Lionel Repka, Jack Timmins

HH.   Jean Ratelle, Jacques Plante, Doug Harvey, Danny Belisle, Dennis Patterson

II.   Rick MacLeish, Dave Schultz, John Garrett, Bobby Taylor, Bill Barber, Rejean Lemelin

JJ.   Alain Caron, Jacques Caron, Bill Goldthorpe, Mike Haworth, Gary Sittler

KK.   Al MacNeil, Al Arbour, Garry Unger, Don Cherry, Mike Nykoluk, Gerry Cheevers

LL.   Jim Cowell, Wayne Rivers, Keith Kokkola, John Miszuk, Mike McKegney, Tom O'Toole

MM   Stan Weir, Glen Hanlon, Alf Handrahan, Ron Low, Dale Smedsmo, Brian Spencer

NN.   Howie Young, Brent Meeke, Wayne Hicks, Bob Barlow, Gary Simmons, Harry Shaw

OO.   Wes Jarvis, Rollie Boutin, Mario Lessard, Markus Mattsson, Steve Carlson

PP.   Dale Smedsmo, Willie Trognitz, Floyd Lahace, Mike Keeler, Peter McNamee

QQ   Steve Coates, Dennis Patterson, Pete Peeters, Frank Bathe, Sudsy Settlemyre

RR   Frank Mathers, Don Cherry, Mike Nykoluk, Craig Patrick, Mike Haworth, Wayne Prestage

SS.   Morris Mott, Terry Murray, Dave Dryden, Gordon Koop, Fred Hilts, Rocky Farr

TEAM LOGOS . . .
ANSWERS

A
Nova Scotia Voyageurs (AHL)

B
Quebec Aces (AHL)

C
Cincinnati Swords (AHL)

D
Lethbridge Broncos (WHL) [Jrs.]

E
Chicago Cougars (WHA)

F
Cleveland Crusaders (WHA)

G
Vancouver Blazers (WHA)

I
Los Angeles Sharks (WHA)

H
Moncton Alpines (AHL)

J
New Haven Nighthawks (AHL)

K
Toronto Marlboros (OHL) [Jrs.]

L
Toronto Toros (WHA)

M
Cleveland Barons (AHL)

N
Ottawa Nationals (WHA)

O
Pittsburgh Hornets (AHL)

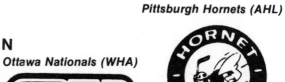

P
Calgary Cowboys (WHA)

Q
Philadelphia Firebirds (NAHL)

R
San Diego Mariners (PHL)

S
Buffalo Bisons (AHL)

T
Grand Rapids Owls (IHL)

U
Niagara Falls Flyers (OHA)

V
Minnesota Fighting Saints (WHA)

W
Philadelphia Rockets (AHL)

X
London Knights (OHL)

Y
Cincinnati Stingers (WHA)

Z
Atlanta Flames (NHL)

AA
Spokane Flyers (PHL)

BB
Indianapolis Racers (WHA)

CC
Cleveland Barons (NHL)

DD
New York Golden Blades (WHA)

EE
New York Raiders (WHA)

FF
Fredericton Express (AHL)

GG
Ft. Wayne Komets (IHL)

HH
Baltimore Clippers (AHL)

II
Richmond Robins (AHL)

JJ
Syracuse Blazers (NAHL)

KK
Rochester Americans (AHL)

MM
Tulsa Oilers (CHL)

LL
San Francisco Shamrocks (PHL)

NN
Phoenix Roadrunners (WHL)

OO
Birmingham South Stars (CHL)

QQ
Maine Mariners (AHL)

PP
Tucson Rustlers (PHL)

RR
Hershey Bears (AHL)

SS
Salt Lake Golden Eagles (WHL)

PART IV

ARENAS . . . THE "TEMPLES" OF HOCKEY

Ask any hockey player where "home" is and, as likely as not, he'll say, "The rink." From the time he first laces on a pair of skates until the day he retires from the game, a hockey player feels most comfortable when he is close to the ice. His true home is the arena in which he and his team plays their games. For that reason, hockey arenas tend to take on the character of the men who play in them, as if each were an extension of the other. They are forever a part of each other even long after he has skated his last shift or the "rink" no longer stands.

The questions which follow all have something to do with hockey arenas, the "temples" in which the game is played. No matter how grand or humble, each is filled with its own special memories.

1 The names of hockey arenas are often more colorful than those of the teams that play in them. What teams have called the following twenty-six arenas "home," and where is each located?

A. Ak-Sar-Ben Arena
B. The Scope
C. Cobo Hall
D. The Myriad
E. Centrum (née Cherry Hill Arena)
F. Central Maine Youth Center
G. Queens Park Arena
H. Assembly Center
I. Hobart Arena
J. Oak Creek Arena
K. The Salt Palace
L. Cumberland County Civic Center
M. Industrial Mutual Association Sports Arena
N. Allen County Memorial Coliseum
O. Snively Rink
P. Onondaga County War Memorial
Q. Luzhniki Stadium
R. The Summit
S. The Big "E" Coliseum
T. The Spectrum
U. The Agridome
V. The Cow Palace
W. The Omni
X. The Yellowstone Metra
Y. Garden City Arena
Z. Cambria County Veterans Memorial Auditorium

2 Twenty-six cities have been represented in the NHL since expansion in 1967, but regular-season games have been played in no less than thirty-three different arenas. What are the names of those buildings, where are they located, and which teams have played "home" games in them?

3 While professional ice hockey is considered an indoor sport, one NHL team could play their home games "under the stars"—if they wished—without moving! Which team is it, and why?

4 The buildings in which NHL teams play are often used for other sporting events in addition to hockey. Basketball, lacrosse, soccer, wrestling, tennis, and horse shows are all frequent attractions in many NHL arenas. One NHL rink, however, was once also the site of an NFL Championship *football* game! Which current NHL rink has that distinction, when and between what two NFL teams was the game played, and why was it contested in a hockey arena?

5 Between which two buildings housing NHL teams do thousands of people travel every day of the year without ever setting foot out-of-doors?

6 Which current NHL arenas have appreciably increased their seating capacities since 1967?

7 Three of the twenty-one arenas in the NHL have ice *surfaces* which do *not* conform to the specifications in the league rulebook. In which buildings are they located and what is wrong with them?

8 NHL playing rules require that the penalty benches be located on the opposite side of the ice from the player benches. But this is not the case in four NHL arenas. Which ones are they and why do they not conform to the rulebook?

9 Why is the center-ice red line in some buildings painted as a checkered line, as opposed to the blue lines, which are always solid?

10 Since expansion, which NHL teams have played *home* games in arenas located in cities *other* than the ones they represent?

11 For many years, the announced sell-out crowd at one NHL arena was almost always as many as three or four thousand less than the actual number of crazed fans packing every corner of the building every game night. Which building was it, and why was the actual attendance always understated?

12 Which two NHL arenas are the farthest apart? And the closest?

13 Most ice surfaces in the NHL are located at, or somewhat below, the surrounding street level. One, however, is considerably above. In which building is it, and how high above the street is its ice surface located?

14 As of the 1983-84 season, which current buildings have served continuously as home ice for active teams in each of the following leagues for the longest period of time? And which ones have the shortest continuous service?

National Hockey League	Central Hockey League
American Hockey League	International Hockey League

15 In which current or past NHL arenas were the following Democrat or Republican National Conventions held?
A) Republicans, 1952
B) Democrats, 1960
C) Republicans, 1976
D) Democrats, 1976
E) Republicans, 1980
F) Democrats, 1980

16 Which two NHL teams needed no less than *five* arenas to play a single season series, how many games did they play against each other in each of the five venues, and why did they move so often? (The series was played since expansion.)

17 Which arena that has been the home of professional hockey teams in three different leagues since 1972 has also been the site of appearances by both the Metropolitan Opera and the Pope?

ARENAS . . . ANSWERS

1 Here are the locations and teams of the twenty-six arenas (cities first.)
A. **Omaha, NE**—Omaha Knights (IHL, CHL) [Ak-Sar-Ben is Nebraska backwards]
B. **Norfolk, VA**—Virginia Red Wings, Tidewater Red Wings, Hampton Gulls (all AHL)
C. **Detroit, MI**—Michigan Stags (WHA)
D. **Oklahoma City, OK**—Oklahoma City Blazers (CHL); Stars (CHL)
E. **Cherry Hill, NJ**—Jersey Larks (EHL); Devils (EHL); Knights (WHA); Aces (NEHL)
F. **Lewiston, ME**—Maine Nordiques (NAHL) [Also Clay-Liston heavyweight title fight]
G. **New Westminster, BC**—New Westminster Bruins (WHL Jrs.)
H. **Tulsa, OK**—Tulsa Oilers (CHL)
I. **Troy, OH**—Troy Bruins (IHL)
J. **Des Moines, IA**—Des Moines Oak Leafs (IHL); Capitols (IHL)
K. **Salt Lake City, UT**—Salt Lake Golden Eagles (WHL, CHL)
L. **Portland, ME**—Maine Mariners (AHL)
M. **Flint, MI**—Flint Generals (IHL)
N. **Ft. Wayne, IN**—Ft. Wayne Komets (IHL)

O. **Durham, NH**—University of New Hampshire Wildcats (NCAA-ECAC)

P. **Syracuse, NY**—Syracuse Warriors (AHL); Braves (EPHL); Blazers (EHL, NAHL); Eagles (AHL); Firebirds (AHL)

Q. **Moscow, USSR**—Moskva Dynamo; Moskva Spartak; Krylia Sovietov; Central Red Army

R. **Houston, TX**—Houston Aeros (WHA)

S. **Springfield, MA**—Springfield Indians (AHL), Kings (AHL)

T. **Philadelphia, PA**—Philadelphia Flyers (NHL)

U. **Regina, SA**—Regina Pats (WHL Jrs.)

V. **San Francisco, CA**—San Francisco Seals (WHL); California Seals (WHL); Oakland Seals (NHL); San Francisco Shamrocks (PHL)

W. **Atlanta, GA**—Atlanta Flames (NHL)

X. **Billings, MT**—Billings Bighorns (WHL Jrs.); Montana Magic (CHL)

Y. **St. Catherines, Ontario**—St. Catherines Black Hawks (OHA Jrs.); Saints (AHL)

Z. **Johnstown, PA**—Johnstown Bluebirds (EHL); Jets (IHL, EHL, NAHL); Wings (NEHL); Charlestown Chiefs (Federal Hockey League)—the mythical team in the movie, "SLAPSHOT" (1976)

2 Here are the thirty-three arenas in which NHL games have been played since 1967.

Boston Garden, Boston, MA (Boston Bruins)

Byrne Meadowlands Arena, East Rutherford, NJ (New Jersey Devils)

Capital Centre, Landover, MD (Washington Capitals)

Chicago Stadium, Chicago, IL (Chicago Black Hawks)

Civic Arena, Pittsburgh, PA (Pittsburgh Penguins)

Civic Center Coliseum, Hartford, CT (Hartford Whalers)

Le Colisee, Quebec City, PQ (Philadelphia Flyers, Quebec Nordiques)

The Cow Palace, San Francisco, CA (Oakland Seals)

Crosby-Kemper Arena, Kansas City, MO (Kansas City Scouts)

The Forum, Inglewood, CA (Los Angeles Kings)

The Forum, Montreal, PQ (Montreal Canadiens)

Joe Louis Arena, Detroit, MI (Detroit Red Wings)

Long Beach Arena, Long Beach, CA (Los Angeles Kings)

Los Angeles Memorial Sports Arena, Los Angeles, CA (Los Angeles Kings)

Madison Square Garden (50th St.), New York, NY (New York Rangers)

Madison Square Garden (34th St.), New York, NY (New York Rangers, Philadelphia Flyers)

Maple Leaf Gardens, Toronto, Ontario (Toronto Maple Leafs, Philadelphia Flyers)

McNichols Arena, Denver, CO (Colorado Rockies)

Memorial Auditorium, Buffalo, NY (Buffalo Sabres)

Metropolitan Sports Center, Bloomington, MN (Minnesota North Stars)

Nassau County Veterans Coliseum, Uniondale (L.I.), NY (New York Islanders)

Northlands Coliseum, Edmonton, Alberta (Edmonton Oilers)
Oakland-Alameda County Coliseum, Oakland, CA (Oakland/California Golden Seals)
Olympia Stadium, Detroit, MI (Detroit Red Wings)
The Omni, Atlanta, GA (Atlanta Flames)
Pacific (PNE) Coliseum, Vancouver, B.C. (Vancouver Canucks)
Richfield Coliseum, Richfield, OH (Cleveland Barons)
The Saddledome, Calgary, Alberta (Calgary Flames)
St. Louis Arena, St. Louis, MO (St. Louis Blues)
The Spectrum, Philadelphia, PA (Philadelphia Flyers)
Springfield Civic Center, Springfield, MA (Hartford Whalers)
The Stampede Corral, Calgary, Alberta (Calgary Flames)
Winnipeg Arena, Winnipeg, Manitoba (Winnepeg Jets)

3 The **Civic Arena,** home ice of the **Pittsburgh Penguins,** has a sectional domed roof which can be rolled back to open the building to the sky. The largest building of its type in the world, the "Igloo's" pie-shaped sections have been retracted during the summer for tennis matches, theatrical performances, and concerts.

4 **Chicago Stadium,** home of the Chicago Black Hawks since 1929, was the site of the play-off game between the **Chicago Bears** and **Portsmouth (OH) Spartans** which decided the NFL championship in 1932. The two teams finished the season tied for first place and met in Chicago on December 18, 1932, to break the deadlock in a one-game play-off. Because of sub-zero weather, the game was moved inside to Chicago Stadium, where it was played on a 60-yard dirt field. The Bears won the game, 9-0, on a touchdown by "Red" Grange.

5 **Madison Square Garden** (New York Rangers) and **Boston Garden** (Boston Bruins) are both built on top of railroad stations. MSG sits atop Pennsylvania Station, while Boston Garden is built over North Station. Both stations are main stops on Amtrak's Northeast corridor, with many trains running between them daily.

6 **Four** NHL arenas have increased their seating capacities since 1967 and **three** others did the same when their tenant teams moved to the NHL from the WHA. **The Spectrum** in Philadelphia added a third deck in the summer of 1972, which increased the building's capacity from 14,262 to 16,600. (The building is currently listed at 17,147 with the addition in recent years of boxes and some other seating.) **Buffalo's Memorial Auditorium,** a veteran AHL arena, added a third tier of approximately 5,000 seats when the Sabres joined the NHL and currently is listed at 16,433. Pittsburgh's **Civic Arena** sat 12,580 when the Penguins entered the NHL but increased that to 16,033 with the addition of a pair of end-rink balconies. The **St. Louis Arena** had 14,500 seats when the Blues entered the NHL in 1967 but increased that to 17,968 in 1970 with a third tier. **Le Colisee** in Quebec City, the **Hartford**

Civic Center Coliseum, and the **Winnipeg Arena** all increased their seating capacities significantly when the Nordiques, Whalers, and Jets joined the NHL from the WHA in 1979. (Hartford's expansion was part of the reconstruction of the building after its roof collapsed in a snowstorm on January 18, 1978.)

7 Rule 2(a) sets the size of the playing surface for NHL rinks at **200 x 85** feet but three arenas are smaller. **Chicago Stadium** is the smallest at 185 x 85, followed by **Boston Garden** at 191 x 83 (the only rink which is not the regulation width), and **Buffalo Memorial Auditorium** at 196 x 85. Rule 3(a) requires that the attacking and defending zones be a standard seventy feet from blue line to end boards. Therefore, all of the missing rink area in the three shorter rinks is taken out of the center neutral zone.

8 **Boston Garden, The Forum (**Montreal), **Le Colisee** (Quebec), and the **Winnipeg Arena** all have their penalty benches located on the same side of the ice as the home team's bench and opposite the visitor's bench. (This gives the home team an obvious advantage in replacing a player who finishes serving a penalty, as he has a much shorter distance to go to reach his bench than a visiting player does.) Boston and Montreal are old buildings and were allowed to remain as they were when the rule was established, i.e., they were "grandfathered" in. Le Colisee and the Winnipeg Arena, both older buildings, were given similar dispensation when the Nordiques and Jets, their tenant clubs, entered the NHL from the WHA in 1979. From 1980 to 1983, there was a fifth non-conforming building, the Stampede Corral in Calgary. Also a veteran building, it was allowed to remain unchanged when the Flames made it their new home when they moved from Atlanta. The club moved into a new building, the Saddledome, at the start of the 1983-84 season.

9 In the early days of television, the center-ice red line was checkered so that **TV** viewers could distinguish it from the blue lines on black and white telecasts. Some buildings have left it that way since the advent of color television broadcasting of hockey games.

10 **Six** NHL teams have played home games in arenas located in cities other than those they represent since 1967. The **Los Angeles Kings** played at the Long Beach Arena in **Long Beach, CA,** while they waited for their permanent home, The Forum, to be completed. (They also played some games at the Los Angeles Memorial Sports Arena.) They moved into The Forum in January, 1968, which is actually located in **Inglewood, CA,** a city situated in the *county* of Los Angeles but not the *city* of Los Angeles. The **Cleveland Barons** played their home games in the Richfield Coliseum in **Richfield, OH,** located about twenty-five miles from Cleveland, and about halfway to Akron.

For their first half-season in the NHL, the **Hartford Whalers** not only didn't play in Hartford, they didn't even play their home games in

Connecticut. Their arena, the Civic Center Coliseum, was still being rebuilt after its roof collapsed (January 18, 1978) when the Whalers joined the NHL. At that time, they were playing their home games at the Springfield Civic Center in **Springfield, MA,** where they had also spent their last season-and-a-half in the WHA. They re-opened the Coliseum on February 6, 1980, two years and 19 days after the roof collapsed. Early in their career, the **Oakland Seals** played some games at the venerable Cow Palace in **San Francisco** in an effort to improve attendance. The **Washington Capitals** have never played a game in Washington, D.C., where no hockey arena exists. The Capital Centre is located in **Landover, MD.**

Like the Whalers, the **Philadelphia Flyers** were sent out of town in their first year in the NHL because of problems with the roof of their building. On March 1, 1968, a windstorm blew part of the roof of the Spectrum away and the City ordered the building closed until repairs and inspections could be made. The Flyers were scheduled to play the New York Rangers at **Madison Square Garden** the next night and then return home to meet the Oakland Seals in a nationally televised game-of-the-week. With the Spectrum closed, it looked as if the game would be cancelled, but the Garden agreed to make their ice available for the game. Anybody who had a ticket for the previous night's Ranger-Flyer game or the Seals-Flyer game scheduled for Philadelphia was admitted free of charge, and 12,127 showed up for the tilt, which ended a 1-1 tie despite a total of 75 shots taken by the two teams. The Flyers continued to play their home games "on the road" for the remainder of the regular season, meeting the Boston Bruins at **Maple Leaf Gardens** and moving the rest of their home games to **Le Colisee** in **Quebec City,** home of their then AHL farm club, the Quebec Aces.

11 The Chicago Fire Marshall restricted the capacity of **Chicago Stadium** to 16,666, but the Black Hawks didn't—except in "official" attendance reports. Current seating capacity of the cavernous hockey hall is now listed at 17,263, and the largest announced crowd (now given accurately) was 20,960 who packed the Stadium on April 10, 1982, to see the Hawks play the Minnesota North Stars.

12 The greatest distance between NHL arenas is the **2,628** miles that separate the **Forum** (Inglewood, CA) and **Le Colisee** (Quebec City, PQ.) The closest are the **Byrne Meadowlands Arena** (East Rutherford, NJ) and **Madison Square Garden** (New York City), which are about four miles apart. In fact if it were not for the buildings of Manhattan, you could see each arena from the roof of the other.

13 **Madison Square Garden,** home of the New York Rangers, has its ice surface located on the **fifth floor** of the building—approximately sixty feet above 34th Street and Eighth Avenue.

14 As of the 1983-84 season, the **Montreal Forum** was the oldest NHL building, having hosted its first league game on **November 29, 1924,** when the Canadiens defeated the Toronto St. Pats, 7-1. **Boston Garden** is the runner-up, opening for hockey on **November 20, 1928** (Montreal 1, Boston 0), followed by **Chicago Stadium,** which opened on **November 16, 1929,** as the Black Hawks defeated the Pittsburgh Pirates, 3-1. The newest NHL building is the **Saddledome,** which replaced the Stampede Corral as home of the Calgary Flames at the start of the **1983-84** season.

Hersheypark Arena, the cozy home of the Hershey Bears, is the senior arena in the American Hockey League. Currently the league's senior franchise, the Bears joined the AHL in the circuit's third season (1938-39) and has played out of the Arena ever since. Nestled in a corner of Hersheypark, a very popular amusement park, the 7,286-seat building is a Hershey Bar's toss from the world-famous chocolate factory where every Hershey Bar is made.

The **Garden City Arena** in St. Catherines, Ontario, is the shortest in point of AHL service. The St. Catherines Saints joined the league in 1982 and played their first game in the Arena on **October 10, 1982,** against the Baltimore Skipjacks.

After 19 seasons in the **Assembly Center,** the Central Hockey League's senior club, the Tulsa Oilers, moved at the start of the 1983-84 season to the **Expo Square Pavillion,** making both that building and the **Yellowstone Metra** in Billings, MT, home of the new Montana Magic, the two newest arenas in the CHL. With the Assembly Center no longer eligible, the current senior building in the CHL is the **Salt Palace,** home ice of the Salt Lake Golden Eagles. The Eagles first played in the 11,000-seat arena in 1969 as a member of the Western Hockey League and continued in that circuit until it folded after the 1973-74 season. They joined the CHL the following fall and continued to play in the Salt Palace.

The **Allen County Memorial Coliseum** in Ft. Wayne, IN, has been the home of the Ft. Wayne Komets since that team entered the IHL in the 1952-53 season. While its 8,032 seats have been filled hundreds of times over during the past three decades, the Memorial Coliseum is also famous throughout much of the rest of North America to radio hockey listeners. As Foster Hewitt did for so many years from the gondola at Maple Leaf Gardens, Komets play-by-play broadcaster **Bob Chase** has described IHL action at the Coliseum from his perch at "radio rinkside" for those same thirty seasons over WOWO-AM [1190 KHz]. The station is a 50,000-watt, clear-channel outlet that can be heard at night from Florida to Hudson's Bay, and has brought action from the "I" to countless listeners (ourselves included) on many a cold winter's night. The **Peoria Prancers** joined the IHL at the start of the 1982-83 season and play their games in the circuit's newest building, the **Peoria Civic Center,** one of the most attractive and modern new buildings in hockey at any level.

15. A. **The Cow Palace,** San Francisco, CA (Eisenhower & Nixon)
   B. **Los Angeles Memorial Sports Arena,** Los Angeles, CA (Kennedy & Johnson)
   C. **Crosby-Kemper Arena,** Kansas City, MO (Ford & Dole)
   D. **Madison Square Garden,** New York, NY (Carter & Mondale)
   E. **Joe Louis Arena,** Detroit, MI (Reagan & Bush)
   F. **Madison Square Garden,** New York, NY (Carter & Mondale)

16 The **Philadelphia Flyers** and **Los Angeles Kings** played their ten-game season series in **1967-68,** their first year in the league, in **five** different arenas. They met each other the first time on the Kings' opening night at the **Long Beach Arena,** Long Beach, CA, on October 11, 1967, a 4-2 Kings' victory. They played in Long Beach because the Kings' new arena, the Forum, was not yet finished. The next building they played in was the **Spectrum** in Philadelphia, where the Flyers beat the Kings, 7-2, on November 26th. The teams' next meeting came at the **Los Angeles Memorial Sports Arena,** another temporary venue, on December 8th, and ended as a 3-0 shut-out in favor of Philadelphia. Three weeks later they met again. This time it was opening night at the **Forum,** December 30, 1967, and the Flyers earned another shut-out, 2-0. They played again the next night, New Year's Eve, at the Spectrum with the Flyers winning again, 9-1. They met again at the Spectrum on January 28th (2-0, Kings) and the Forum on February 16·(7-1, Kings). Their eighth meeting was again at the Spectrum on February 29, 1967, in a 3-1 Los Angeles victory. It turned out to be the last regular season game the Flyers would play there that year, as the roof blew off in a windstorm the next day.

   With the Flyers forced to play the rest of their home schedule "on the road," the two teams met in the fifth different building that season on March 14 at **Le Colisee** in Quebec City, PQ, then the home of the Flyers' AHL farm club, the Quebec Aces. (The building now is home ice for the NHL Quebec Nordiques.) Both the Flyers' Bernie Parent and the Kings' Terry Sawchuk, two of the greatest goalies in the history of the game, earned shut-outs that evening as the game ended in a scoreless (0-0) tie. The tenth and final meeting came at the Forum on March 23, a 4-2 Kings' victory. Since that first season, the Kings and Flyers have never played each other in buildings other than the Forum and Spectrum.

17 **Civic Center Convention Hall** in Philadelphia, PA. was the home of the WHA Philadelphia Blazers (1972-73) and the Philadelphia Firebirds (NAHL, 1974-77; AHL, 1977-79). The Met used Convention Hall for one week in the early 1970's when it made it a stop on its annual Spring Tour. Pope John Paul II also used the same arena for a public audience when he visited the United States in 1979.

SUPER QUESTION FOUR: "YOU MEAN THAT'S NOT HIS REAL NAME?!"

F or the most part, the given names of hockey players, coaches, and builders are as familiar as their surnames. But not always! For our fourth Super Question, we are giving you the real given names of twenty-six well-known hockey personalities, names not usually associated with the men they belong to. Your task is to identify them by the name under which each made his fame in hockey. After you have identified as many as you can from their real given names alone, turn to the next section of this Super Question, where we have provided a clue to the identity of each man.

A. Gerhard Otto
B. Constantine Falkland Kerrys
C. Allister Wences
D. Nicholas Evampios
E. Modere
F. Mikolaj Nickolas
G. Woodrow Wilson Clarence
H. Calvin Pearly
I. Armand
J. Frederick John Charles
K. Courtney Keith
L. Frederick Arthur (full name)
M. Ivanhoe

N. Francis William
O. Juha Markku
P. Francis Michael
Q. Hubert Jacques
R. Thore Robert
S. Gordon Arthur
T. John Wayne
U. William Barton
V. John Calverley
W. Garnet Edward
X. Joseph Jacques Omer
Y. Wilhelm Heinrich
Z. Anthony Syiiyd

THE CLUES

Now that you have gone through the list of unfamiliar real given names of our twenty-six hockey personalities, here is your clue to each man's identity.

A. A longtime Philadelphia winger who moved from his favorite spot in the other team's crease to the Hockey Night in Canada broadcast booth.
B. He once said: "If you can't beat them in the alley, you can't beat them on the ice."
C. He coached one of the five NHL teams he earlier played for to a Stanley Cup.
D. This popular winger plays just a ferryboat-ride away from his birthplace.
E. His goal broke a scoreless tie to end the longest game in NHL history.
F. He came from Drohiczyn, Poland, to play five NHL seasons with Pittsburgh and St. Louis.
G. He spent fifteen seasons in Boston, where he played on an legendary line.
H. A member of the "Atomic Line," he was followed to the NHL by two sons.
I. He later coached the club he played for at age 16 to the Stanley Cup finals.

J.   This red-headed right wing played for four NHL clubs in the 1970's.

K.   A greyhound on defense, he won Stanley Cups both as a player and General Manager.

L.   A son of the Earl of Derby, he donated a trophy which carries his name.

M.   A native of Val D'or, PQ, he was an IHL player with Toledo, Lansing, and Ft. Wayne.

N.   An offer of $1,000,000 for his contract was once turned down in the 1960's by the team of this forward, who is one of the game's all-time great scorers.

O.   A long-time center in Los Angeles, his nine-year career included two other NHL stops.

P.   This man's half-century plus NHL career includes service as player, referee and coach.

Q.   Included in one of the NHL's biggest trades, he played 17 seasons with four clubs.

R.   He is second only to Rocket Richard in Stanley Cup overtime goals, one of which was a Cup-winner, while averaging less than 25 goals per year in his career.

S.   Now a coach, he once scored six goals in an NHL game as a player.

T.   A defenseman with Detroit, California, and Minnestoa.

U.   Once called the "Bobby Orr of the WHA," he also played for three NHL clubs.

V.   Eddie Shore once traded this NHL veteran GM for a set of goal nets.

W.   This winger played for Boston, Detroit, St. Louis, and Washington in ten NHL seasons.

X.   He introduced a now-standard piece of hockey equipment during his Hall of Fame career.

Y.   A first-round draftee from the Hamilton Fincups, he is one of the NHL's biggest players.

Z.   This Montreal native was drafted by Buffalo but almost played for the WHA Birmingham Bulls instead.

MYSTERY PLAYER E

THE ANSWERS

Here are the names that the twenty-six players with unfamiliar real given names became famous under.

A. **Gary** (Gerhard Otto) **Dornhoefer**
B. **Conn** (Constantine Falkland Kerrys) **Smythe**
C. **Al** (Allister Wences) **MacNeil**
D. **Nick** (Nicholas Evampios) **Fotiu**
E. (Modere) **"Mud" Bruneteau**
F. **Nick** (Mikolaj Nickolas) **Harbaruk**
G. (Woodrow Wilson Clarence) **"Porky" Dumart**
H. **Cal** (Calvin Pearly) **Gardner**
I. (Armand) **"Bep" Guidolin**
J. (Frederick John Charles) **"Buster" Harvey**
K. **Keith** (Courtney Keith) **Allen**
L. (Frederick Arthur), **Lord Stanley of Preston**
M. **Ivan** (Ivanhoe) **Belisle**
N. **Frank** (Francis William) **Mahovlich**
O. (Juha Markku) **"Whitey" Widing**
P. (Francis Michael) **"King" Clancy**
Q. (Hubert Jacques) **"Pit" Martin**
R. **Bobby** (Thore Robert) **Nystrom**
S. (Gordon Arthur) **"Red" Berenson**
T. **Wayne** (John Wayne) **Muloin**
U. **Bart** (William Barton) **Crashley**
V. (John Calverley) **"Jake" Milford**
W. (Garnet Edward) **"Ace" Bailey**
X. **Jacques** (Joseph Jacques Omer) **Plante**
Y. **Willie** (Wilhelm Heinrich) **Huber**
Z. **Tony** (Anthony Syiiyd) **McKegney**

PART V

"CANADA, UNITED STATES, SOVIET UNION AND. . ."
ICE CHIPS II

 ere's our second dose of miscellaneous hockey brainteasers for you.

1 Since ice hockey was first played as an Olympic sport in 1920, only four countries have won the Gold Medal in Hockey. Canada, the United States, and the Soviet Union are three of them. What is the only *other* country to win an Olympic ice hockey championship?

2 Who was the last player cut from the 1960 U.S. Olympic Hockey Team before the VIII Winter Olympic Games at Squaw Valley, CA, in which that club won the Gold Medal for the United States for the first time?

3 A total of fifteen American-born Olympic medalists have played in the NHL since the 1980 Winter Olympic Games. Of those fifteen, all but *two* were members of the 1980 U.S. team. Who are the two American-born Olympic medalists who have played in the NHL since 1980 who did *not* also play in the 1980 games, and what NHL teams have they played for?

4 Who was the first player to wear Phil Esposito's famous number 7 with the Boston Bruins after Espo was traded to the New York Rangers? (It wasn't Ray Bourque.)

5 The average total number of penalty minutes called in a professional hockey game against both teams is about thirty. The fewest number called, obviously, is zero and that happens very rarely. Within thirty minutes, what is the *greatest* number of penalty minutes called in a regular season or play-off professional hockey game in North America?

6 Over the years, hockey teams have occasionally changed their nicknames while remaining in the same city. Under what other names have these currently active professional franchises previously played? (Some have changed names more than once.)

A. Toronto Maple Leafs (NHL)
B. Binghamton Whalers (AHL)
C. Detroit Red Wings (NHL)
D. Springfield Indians (AHL)
E. Hershey Bears (AHL)
F. Muskegon Mohawks (IHL)

7 With three games to play in the 1954-55 season, two teams were tied for first place when they met each other in a game that would likely decide that year's regular season NHL championship. The visiting team won the game that night in the rarest way possible and went on to defeat the same team a few weeks later for the Stanley Cup championship as well. What were the two teams, how was that crucial regular season game won, and why?

8 Al Arbour (St. Louis, New York Islanders), Gerry Cheevers (Boston) and Don Cherry (Boston, Colorado) all had long playing careers before turning to coaching in the NHL. All three, in fact, were once teammates on a club which won both its regular-season and play-off championships, while two of them also won major individual league awards. What was the team, the season, and the trophies these men won?

9 A tradition in virtually every arena in which professional hockey is played is for the media to select "Three Stars" at the end of each game. On the evening of April 1st, 1979, the AHL Hershey Bears defeated the Binghamton Dusters, 6-5, at the Broome County Arena. The three stars voted by the media that night were well deserving of the honor. They were the Bears' Tony McKegney and Bill Riley (each with a goal and an assist) and Binghamton's Mike Marson (two goals). What was unusual about this trio?

10 What NHL coach active during the 1983-84 season was the only player to have ever had his number retired in the 46-year history of the professional team with which he spent most of his playing career?

11 Since 1967, the state of Florida has been the home of four professional hockey franchises, and the state of Georgia, two. What were the names and leagues of these six clubs?

12 During a seven-year period from 1975-76 to 1982-83, Erie, PA, has been represented in professional hockey by a single team, the Erie Blades. That team, however, has played in five different leagues during that span. Name them.

13 When defenseman Larry "The Rock" Zeidel joined the Philadelphia Flyers early in the 1967-68 season, what unofficial NHL record did he set?

14 Through the 1982-83 season, the Stanley Cup has been won by only seven teams based in the United States. Name them.

15 The 1951 Stanley Cup finals were like no other in the history of Cup play. Why?

MYSTERY PLAYER F

ICE CHIPS II . . . ANSWERS

1 The 1936 Winter Olympic Games, held at Garmisch-Partenkirchen, Germany, saw **Great Britain** win the Gold Medal in hockey by defeating Silver Medal-winning Canada, 2-1, playing a scoreless (0-0) tie with the United States (Bronze), and defeating Czechoslovakia, 5-0, in the medal round. One of the members of the British team was Edgar "Chirp" Brenchley, who later emigrated to the United States, where he had a successful career as a minor league player, coach and NHL scout.

2 The last player cut from the 1960 U.S. Olympic Hockey Team was **Herb Brooks,** who went on to become coach of the 1980 Gold Medal-winning U.S. team after a long tenure as coach at the University of Minnesota. In 1981 he was named coach of the NHL New York Rangers.

3 The only two American-born Olympic medalists to play in the NHL since 1980 who were not members of the 1980 U.S. team are defenseman **Mark Howe** and center **Robbie Ftorek.** Since 1980 Howe has played with both the **Hartford Whalers** and the **Philadelphia Flyers,** while Ftorek has performed with the **Quebec Nordiques** and the **New York Rangers.** Both won their Olympic medals at Sapporo, Japan, as members of the 1972 U.S. Olympic Hockey Team that won the Silver Medal in the XI Winter Games. (The Gold went to the USSR, the Bronze to Czechoslovakia.)

Howe was born in Detroit, MI, where his father, Gordie, was playing for the Detroit Red Wings. At 16, Mark was the youngest member of the Olympic team that year. After the Olympics, he returned to play junior hockey with the Toronto Marlboros (OHA) with whom he won a Memorial Cup championship in 1973. He then turned pro with his brother, Marty, and his father (who came out of retirement to play with his sons) and the three played together in the WHA with the Houston Aeros and New England Whalers until the league merged with the NHL in 1979. They played one season together in the NHL with the renamed Hartford Whalers before Gordie retired for good in 1980, at age 52. Mark was traded to the Philadelphia Flyers in June, 1982, and was named to the NHL's First All-Star Team in 1982-83.

Ftorek, a 20-year-old center for the 1972 Olympians, had been a high school hockey star in his native Needham, MA. He turned pro immediately after the Games with the Detroit Red Wings, but he only appeared in fifteen major league games during the two seasons he spent in their organization. (He spent the rest of the time playing for the Wings' AHL development clubs in Virginia.) He jumped to the WHA in 1974, where he played with considerable success and was named the league's Most Valuable Player for the 1976-77 season. He spent his first three WHA seasons (1974-77) with the Phoenix Roadrunners and his last two (1977-79) with the Cincinnati Stingers, and averaged well over

100-points-per-season over that five-year span. He returned to the NHL in 1979 with the Quebec Nordiques (whom he later served as captain), and was traded to the New York Rangers on December 30, 1981.

Four other members of the 1972 U.S. team played in the NHL *before* 1980. They were **Jim McElmury** (Minnesota, Kansas City, and Colorado), **Tom Mellor** (Detroit), **Henry Boucha** (Detroit, Minnesota, Kansas City, and Colorado), and **Tim Sheehy,** who played four years with the WHA Whalers and briefly with the NHL Whalers early in the 1979-80 season.

4 Winger **Sean Shanahan** wore Phil Esposito's famous number **7** when he played briefly with the Bruins during the 1977-78 season, making him the first to wear it after Espo was traded to the New York Rangers on November 7, 1975.

5 On October 14, 1981, referee Bob Henry whistled a total of **520** minutes in penalties in an AHL game between the Adirondack Red Wings and the Hershey Bears played at Hersheypark Arena. (Hershey won, 7-4.) He had already handed out 212 minutes during the game when a brawl broke out with just sixteen-seconds left in the third period. The final 318 minutes were all called at that point including 92 alone against the goalies. It took over one hour to play the final sixteen seconds of the game.

6 Here are the names these teams previously played under:
   A. Toronto Maple Leafs—**Arenas** (1917-1919); **St. Patricks** (1919-1926)
   B. Binghamton Whalers—**Broome Dusters** (1972-1977 [NAHL]; 1977-1980 [AHL])
   C. Detroit Red Wings—**Cougars** (1926-1930); **Falcons** (1930-1933)
   D. Springfield Indians—**Kings** (1967-75)
   E. Hershey Bears—**B'ars** (1932-1936 [EAHL])
   F. Muskegon Mohawks—**Zephyrs** (1960-1965)

7 The **Montreal Canadiens** and **Detroit Red Wings** were tied for first place when they met at the Montreal Forum on March 17, 1955, with three games to go in the season. The game ended that night as a Detroit victory by **forfeit.** Four nights earlier, Maurice "Rocket" Richard had puched linesman Cliff Thompson as the official attempted to break up a fight between Richard and the Bruins' Hal Laycoe during a game at Boston Garden. On the morning of the Detroit game (which also happened to be St. Patrick's Day), NHL President Clarence Campbell announced Richard would be suspended not only for the three remaining games of the season, but for the entire *playoffs* as well. This, of course, did not sit too well with the Montreal fans. That night the Wings were leading, 4-1, when Mr. Campbell arrived at the Forum and took his customary seat at rinkside. His arrival was enough to remove tha last restraint on the crowd's emotions and soon the arena was littered with

bottles, bricks, and tomatoes. The game could not be continued and was forfeited to Detroit. The riot, meanwhile, spilled out into the streets of Montreal and lasted much of the night.

Richard's suspension cost him the only NHL trophy that he failed to win during his glorious career, the Art Ross. Teammate Bernie "Boom Boom" Geoffrion passed him during those final three games to capture the league scoring championship. Several weeks later the Canadiens and Wings met in the Stanley Cup finals, which Detroit won, four games to three. The Canadiens, however, won the Cup the next five years in a row.

8 Al Arbour, Gerry Cheevers, and Don Cherry were all members of the **1964-65 Rochester Americans** when the club won both the AHL's regular season and Calder Cup play-off championships. Cheevers played all 72 regular-season games for the Americans, allowing just 199 goals for a 2.68 goals-against average (five shut-outs) and a record of 48-21-3. He and the Americans were 8-2 in the play-offs, defeating Quebec and Hershey for the Calder Cup. Cheevers won the Hap Holmes Trophy as the league's top goalie for 1964-65, while Arbour captured the **Eddie Shore Plaque** as Defenseman of the Year.

9 The "Three Stars" that night—Tony McKegney, Bill Riley, and Mike Marson—are all **black.**

10 Toronto Maple Leafs head coach **Mike Nykoluk** is the only player to ever have his number retired in the 46-year history of the AHL **Hershey Bears.** Nykoluk wore number **8** during his fourteen seasons with the Bears, and is the fourth all-time leading scorer in the AHL, with **881** career points.

11 Since 1967, the state of Florida has been the home of the EHL **Jacksonville Rockets,** SHL **Suncoast Suns,** AHL **Jacksonville Barons** and the WHA **Miami Screaming Eagles.** (While the WHA franchise was awarded, a team never played as it was cancelled by the league before the season got under way for failure to meet financing requirements.) Georgia's two franchises were the NHL **Atlanta Flames,** and the SHL **Macon Whoopies.** (The Whoopies played about two-thirds of the 1973-74 season in the SHL before folding. They wore Montreal Canadien uniforms with their own logo.)

12 The Erie Blades have played in the **North American Hockey League, Northeastern Hockey League, Eastern Hockey League, American Hockey League,** and the **Atlantic Coast Hockey League.**

13 After playing with the Stanley Cup champion Detroit Red Wings in 1951-52 and the Chicago Black Hawks two years later, Larry Zeidel spent his next fourteen seasons playing in the American and Western Hockey Leagues. When he joined the NHL Philadelphia Flyers in 1967, it was his first NHL action in **fourteen years**—the longest such hiatus between stints in league history.

14 The only U.S.-based teams to win the Stanley Cup through the 1982-83 season are (working backwards) the **New York Islanders, Philadelphia Flyers, Boston Bruins, Chicago Black Hawks, Detroit Red Wings, New York Rangers,** and (in 1916-17) the **Seattle Metropolitans.**

15 Every game in the five-game 1951 Stanley Cup finals was decided in **overtime.** Here is a summary of the five games and the overtime goal-scorers in the series which was won by the Toronto Maple Leafs over the Montreal Canadiens, four games to one:

Game 1) Montreal 2 at TORONTO 3 (Sid Smith, 5:51) [April 11, 1951]
Game 2) MONTREAL 3 at Toronto 2 (Maurice Richard, 2:55) [April 14, 1951]
Game 3) TORONTO 2 at Montreal 1 (Ted Kennedy, 4:47) [April 17, 1951]
Game 4) TORONTO 3 at Montreal 2 (Harry Watson, 5:15) [April 19, 1951]
Game 5) Montreal 2 at TORONTO 3 (Bill Barilko, 2:53) [April 21, 1951]

SUPER QUESTION FIVE: FROM 16 to 68 . . . THE NHL'S YOUNGEST & OLDEST

O ur fifth Super Question challenge for you is one to test the very best of hockey trivia minds. Listed below are ten NHL milestones or accomplishments that have each been achieved by many players over the history of the league. Your job is to identify both the youngest and the oldest player to do each. This is not an easy question and it should take you some time to eliminate possible answers in many of the ten sections. After you have given it a good shot you may turn to the clue section of this Super Question. There we have given you a clue to the identity of each pair of answers.

Here are our ten "Youngest and Oldest" catagories:
A. Winner of a Major NHL Award
B. Member of an Official NHL First All-Star Team (End of Season)
C. Playing Member of a Stanley Cup Championship Team
D. NHL Player (Appearance in an NHL game)
E. NHL Rookie (Appearance in his first NHL game)
F. Winner of the Calder Memorial Trophy (NHL Rookie of the Year)
G. Coach in an NHL Game (Head coach behind the bench)
H. Single Season 50-Goal Scorer
I. Single Season 100-Point Scorer
J. Winner of the Hart Trophy (NHL Most Valuable Player)

THE CLUES

Now that you have had a chance test your memory on the NHL's youngest and oldest in each of our ten categories, we now offer you a clue to help you determine the identity of those you did not get. Each pair of clues tells you something about the two players, but the order of the clues is arbitrary, i.e., we are not telling you which one is which by the order of the clues in each duo. You should also take into consideration the possibility that a single player may be the answer to more than one question.

A. One major award-winner used to pass his time between Stanley Cup championships by knitting. The other was a member of an Ontario-based junior team that won a Memorial Cup championship before joining the NHL.

B. Former NHL center Terry Crisp used to refer affectionately to one of these men as: "The other guy from Parry Sound." The other All-Star was named to the First Team seven times in his career.

C. The Red Deer Rustlers sent one of these Stanley Cup championship players to the NHL. The other was honored by both the NHL and WHL which named trophies for him.

D. One player was an NHL teammate of his son's, the other later coached Bobby Orr with the Oshawa Generals.

E. One rookie later coached both the Edmonton Oilers and Philadelphia Firebirds. The WHL career penalty minute record (1,744) belonged to the other.

F. The oldest and youngest winners of the rookie award won it in consecutive years.

G. One NHL coach played pro hockey for the Charlotte Checkers and later became a TV broadcaster. The other both played and officiated in the league before coaching.

H. Indiana was where one NHL 50-goal scorer started his pro career while the other first played pro hockey in Edmonton—with the Flyers.

I. Both players also hold the same 100-point record in the WHA record book.

J. The Montreal Canadiens sported one of these players as an All-Star left winger for many years. The other signed the longest contract in NHL history.

MYSTERY PLAYER G

THE ANSWERS

Here are the players who were the youngest and oldest men in each NHL category. In order to have a point of reference for the awards' categories, we have used June 1st as the date for each season's announcement of winners.

A. The youngest NHL award-winner was **Dale Hawerchuck** of the Winnipeg Jets who won the Calder Memorial Trophy as the Rookie of the Year in 1982 at age **19 years, 26 days.** Bobby Orr was second at 19 years, 72 days when he won the 1967 Calder Trophy. Wayne Gretzky won both the Hart and Lady Byng Trophies in his rookie NHL season at age 19 years, 126 days.

   Jacques Plante shared the Vezina Trophy with Glenn Hall as a member of the St. Louis Blues in 1969 at age **40 years, 103 days.**

B. **Bobby Orr** was named to the First All-Star Team in 1967 at age **19 years, 72 days. Glenn Hall** was named First Team All-Star in 1969 at age **37 years, 220 days.**

C. The New York Islanders' **Brent Sutter** was age **19 years, 340 days** when he helped his team win the Stanley Cup on May 16, 1982.

   The New York Rangers won the 1928 Stanley Cup title on April 7, 1928. **Lester Patrick,** played in goal in one final series game beating the Montreal Maroons, 2-1. He was age **45 years, 98 days.**

D. The great **Gordie Howe** had just passed his *52nd* birthday (born March 31, 1928) when he played his last NHL game at the Montreal Forum as the Canadiens eliminated Howe's Hartford Whalers in the first round of the 1980 play-offs.

   Armand "Bep" Guidolin (born December 9, 1925) was **16 years, 9 months** of age when he made his NHL debut with the Boston Bruins in 1942.

E. As noted in the previous answer, "Bep" Guidolin was the youngest player to appear in an NHL game, at age 16 in 1942. All-time WHL badman **Cornelius Dennis "Connie" Madigan** played 20 games for the St. Louis Blues in the 1972-73 season at age **38.** He was born on October 4, 1934.

F. As noted in answer 1, Dale Hawerchuck was the youngest winner of the Calder Memorial Trophy, at **19 years, 26 days,** in 1982. The previous season, Quebec's Peter Stastny was named winner of the Rookie of the Year award in 1981 at age **34 years, 285 days.** The award to an experienced international player raised some eyebrows, since he was allowed to be considered an "NHL rookie" while Wayne Gretzky was classified a veteran in 1979-80 because he had already played in the WHA.

G. Hall of **Famer Frank "King" Clancy** coached the Toronto Maple Leafs in an emergency during the 1971-72 season at 68 years of age. He began his playing career with the Ottawa Senators in 1921 at age 18 and later served as an NHL referee.

Gary Green was age **26 years, 82 days** when he was promoted from the AHL Hershey Bears to become coach of the Washington Capitals on November 14, 1979.

H. **Wayne Gretzky** became the NHL's youngest 50-goal scorer on April 2, 1980 at age **19 years, 65 days,** when he beat Minnesota's Gary Edwards to earn a 1-1 tie at Northlands Coliseum. (His first pro team was the WHA Indianapolis Racers.)

Johnny Bucyk became the NHL's oldest 50-goal scorer at age **35 years, 33 days** when the great Boston Bruin winger beat Detroit's Roy Edwards for his 50th goal of the 1970-71 season on March 16, 1971. (His first pro team was the WHL Edmonton Flyers, with whom he broke in in 1954.)

I. **Wayne Gretzky** is also the NHL's youngest 100-point scorer, at age **19 years, 29 days**—which came on February 24th, 1980.

Gordie Howe notched 100 points in the NHL for his only time in a game at Chicago on March 30, 1969, one day shy of his **41st** birthday.

Wayne Gretzky was the youngest Hart Trophy winner at **19 years, 126 days** when he won the league MVP title for his first time in 1980.

J. **Aurel Joliat** won the Hart Trophy in 1934 at age **32 years, 285 days**. The slight Canadien winger (135 lbs) was elected to the Hall of Fame in 1945. Boston's Phil Esposito is the runner-up, winning the 1974 Hart Trophy at age **32 years, 100 days.**

PART VI

"MINNESOTA DRAFTS . . . THE GOVERNOR" . . . THE WHA

While the NHL's biggest expansion came in 1967 when the six-team circuit doubled in size to twelve clubs, it is fair to say that hockey experienced an even bigger expansion in 1972. That was the debut year of the WHA, the World Hockey Association, which started play with twelve teams spread throughout the United States and Canada. Many teams would come and go during the brief seven-year life of the league, but it would prove to have a lasting impact on both hockey in general and the NHL in particular. Four of the current member clubs of the NHL were also original members of the WHA. The Edmonton Oilers, Winnipeg Jets, Quebec Nordiques and Hartford (née New England) Whalers all joined the NHL in 1979 when the WHA disbanded.

While the level of play in the WHA may have never consistently approached that of the NHL, it was nonetheless an interesting and entertaining league. It often did not feel itself "constrained" by the inertia of tradition which had kept the NHL conservative in its approach to the game. It was a league which was for the most part run by men who had very little experience in running a hockey business, but who knew something about running an entertainment business. Not all of their ideas worked, but it made for a very interesting and memorable seven-year period—the "WHA Era" if you will.

On the following few pages we offer you some serious—and some not so serious—questions about hockey's "other" major league. We hope they provide you with a challenge—and a few smiles.

1 In the WHA's first draft, GM/Coach Glen Sonmor of the Minnesota Fighting Saints drafted the then sitting Governor of Minnesota for his players list. Who was this chief executive of the Saints' home state, and why would they draft him?

2 Which were the ten cities to be awarded original franchises when the WHA was organized on November 1, 1971?

3 Who was the first player to sign an agreement to join a WHA team, and the first to sign a standard player's contract? (They were two different players.)

4 In what "hockey capital" was the first head office of the WHA located?

5 Who signed the WHA's biggest contract in 1972, for how long did it run, what was it worth, and where was it signed?

6 Who signed the WHA's *second* biggest contract in 1972, what was it worth, (and within 100), how many career WHA games did he play in the league between 1972 and 1979?

7 How did the WHA's referee's uniform differ from that of that worn by NHL arbiters?

8 In what arenas did the original 1972 WHA teams play in the league's debut season?

9 Which WHA teams wore the following "official" colors:
A. Jungle Green & Gold
B. Blue with Red & White
C. Powder Blue, Navy Blue & White
D. Royal Blue, New Gold & White
E. Forest Green, White & Black
F. Northern Blue, Red & White
H. Orange, Blue & White
I. Purple, Black & White
J. Red, Black & White
K. Royal Blue, Orange & White
L. Red & White with Blue
M. Orange, Gold & White

10 Of all the original-roster players who were in the WHA when the league made its debut on October 11, 1972, just three played in the NHL during the 1983-84 season. Who were they and what were their WHA and NHL clubs in 1972 and 1984?

11 In addition to the three players in question #10, eight others played in the NHL in 1982-83 who played in the WHA during that league's second season (1973-74). Who were they and what were their WHA and NHL clubs in 1973 and 1983?

12 Four of the ten original franchises awarded on November 1, 1971, either failed to operate or opened the 1972-73 season playing in a city other than the one to which the franchise was first given. What were the four cities and what became of their franchises?

13 Who was the all-time leading scorer in WHA history when the league played its last game in 1979?

14 What was the name of the WHA's play-off championship trophy, and where was it first "retired" to when the league was dissolved in 1979?

15 The WHA Rules in 1972 were similar to those of the NHL, but there were several significant differences. How did they differ in each of the following areas?
A. Tie games
B. The Puck
C. Icing
D. Altercations
E. Sticks

16 What former ticket manager for the NHL Philadelphia Flyers once had a WHA trophy named in his honor?

17 In a fit of humility, the WHA named its award for the league's MVP after the circuit's president. Who was he, who won it the first time, and for whom was the award later renamed?

18 Who was the WHA's all-time leader in penalty minutes, and what NHL clubs did he play for after leaving the WHA?

19 Who were the WHA's eight original referees, and who was the only one to work in the NHL *after* his WHA service?

20 Who were the original twelve coaches behind WHA benches at the start of the 1972-73 season?

MYSTERY PLAYER H

THE WHA . . . ANSWERS

1 Wendell Anderson was then the 36-year-old Governor of Minnesota, but in 1955 he was a promising young hockey player from Minnesota who skated on the 1955 U.S. National Team. While he was certainly not "drafted" with the idea he would ever play for the Saints, it was a brilliant PR move.

2 The cities that were awarded the WHA's ten original franchises on November 1, 1981, were: **Calgary, Chicago, Dayton, Edmonton, Los Angeles, Miami, New York, St. Paul, San Francisco,** and **Winnipeg.**

3 Goalie **Bernie Parent,** then with the Toronto Maple Leafs, signed an agreement to play for the Miami Screaming Eagles on February 27, 1972. In March, 1972, U.S. Olympic goalie **Mike Curran** became the first player to sign a WHA Standard Player's Contract.

4 The WHA's first league office was located in the "hockey capital" of **Santa Ana, California,** where WHA President Gary Davidson, a 38-year old attorney, had his law offices.

5 Bobby Hull signed his ten-year contract worth **$2,750,000** before a crowd of over 10,000 people at the corner of Potage and Main Streets in downtown **Winnipeg, Manitoba. He was presented at that time with a certified check for $1,000,000.**

6 Derek Sanderson, the flamboyant Boston Bruin center, jumped from the defending Stanley Cup champions to sign a **$2,325,000** contract with the **Philadelphia Blazers.** His entire WHA career consisted of **eight games** with the Blazers (3 goals, 3 assists; 69 penalty minutes). Before the season was much more than half over, Sanderson was back with the Bruins. He also played in the NHL with the New York Rangers, St. Louis Blues, Vancouver Canucks, and Pittsburgh Penguins before he retired in 1978.

7 Instead of wearing red armbands on a black and white striped shirt as did NHL referees, WHA refs wore a shirt with alternating vertical **red and white stripes.** WHA linesmen wore black and white striped shirts without armbands, just like NHL linesmen.

8 The WHA's twelve 1972-73 member clubs played their home games in the following fifteen arenas:
Boston Arena (6,000), Boston, MA (New England Whalers)
Boston Garden (14,994), Boston, MA (New England Whalers)
Cleveland Arena (9,500), Cleveland, OH (Cleveland Crusaders)
Le Colisee (10,000), Quebec City, PQ (Quebec Nordiques)
Edmonton Gardens (5,200), Edmonton), Edmonton,
Alberta (Alberta Oilers)
International Amphitheatre (9,000), Chicago, IL (Chicago Cougars)
Long Beach Arena (11,325), Long Beach, CA (Los Angeles Sharks)

Los Angeles Memorial Sports Arena (14,700), Los Angeles, CA (Los Angeles Sharks)
Madison Square Garden (17,250), New York, NY (New York Raiders)
Ottawa Civic Centre (9,300), Ottawa, Ontario (Ottawa Nationals)
Philadelphia Civic Center Convention Hall (9,000), Philadelphia, PA (Philadelphia Blazers)
St. Paul Auditorium (8,000), St. Paul, MN (Minnesota Fighting Saints)
St. Paul Civic Center (16,180), St. Paul, MN (Minnesota Fighting Saints)
Sam Houston Coliseum (9,300), Houston, TX (Houston Aeros)
Winnipeg Arena (11,000), Winnipeg, Manitoba (Winnipeg Jets)

9 Here are the WHA teams which wore the mystery colors in the 1972-73 season:

A. Chicago Cougars
B. Winnipeg Jets
C. Houston Aeros
D. Minnesota Fighting Saints
E. New England Whalers
F. Quebec Nordiques
H. New York Raiders
I. Cleveland Crusaders
J. Los Angeles Sharks
K. Alberta Oilers
L Ottawa Nationals
M. Philadelphia Blazers

10 The only three original-roster WHA players in the NHL during the 1983-84 season were the following:
Richard Brodeur was a rookie goalie from the Cornwall Royals (QMJHL) with the Quebec Nordiques. In 1983-84 he played with the NHL Vancouver Canucks. The Minnesota Fighting Saints had both center **Mike Antonovich** (a rookie from the University of Minnesota) and right wing **Bob MacMillan** (the 20-year old former captain of the OHA St. Catherines Black Hawks) on their 1972-73 roster. In 1983-84, both were again teammates with the NHL New Jersey Devils.

11 The eight additional second-season WHA players in the NHL in 1982-83 were: **Mark Howe** (Houston—Philadelphia Flyers); **Marty Howe** (Houston—Boston Bruins); **Colin Campbell** (Vancouver—Detroit Red Wings); **Rejean Houle** (Quebec—Montreal Canadiens); **Marc Tardiff** (Quebec—Quebec); **Curt Brackenbury** (Chicago—St. Louis); **Pat Hickey** (Toronto—St. Louis); and **John Garrett** (Minnesota—Quebec/Vancouver)

12 **Calgary, Dayton, Miami,** and **San Francisco** were all awarded *original* WHA franchises on November 1, 1971, but no teams operated in those cities when the league played its first games, just three weeks short of a year later. On April 14, 1972, the league notified the owners of the Calgary and Miami clubs that they were in default and had two weeks to get back in good standing. They failed to do so and their franchises were cancelled on April 28th. The other two franchises both moved before the start of league play. San Francisco was sold on February 11, 1972, to a group of businessmen from Quebec City and became the Quebec

Nordiques. In March, the owners of the Dayton Aeros moved the franchise to Houston but retained the nickname Aeros. Therefore, eight of the ten original franchises granted on November 1st survived to play, although two did so in other cities. Four other franchises were granted later to bring the opening season size of the circuit to twelve teams. Ottawa and New England were awarded franchises on November 21st, and Philadelphia and Cleveland were added in June, 1972.

13 Center **Andre Lacroix** was the WHA's all-time leading scorer, with 798 points in regular-season play and 43 in play-off competition. He scored a total of 251 regular season and 14 play-off goals, and assisted on 547 in regular season play (also an all-time league record) and 29 in post-season action. Lacroix also appeared in more WHA games than any other player—551—as well as 48 Avco World Cup games. After just over four years in the NHL with Philadelphia and Chicago, Lacroix was an original-roster WHA player with the Philadelphia Blazers. When the Blazers moved to Vancouver the next season, Lacroix joined the New York Golden Blades, but that club dissolved several weeks into the season. The players became property of the league and were moved to Cherry Hill, NJ, just across the river from Philadelphia, and played the rest of the season as the league-owned Jersey Knights. The next year (1974-75), Lacroix joined the San Diego Mariners and played for them for three seasons. He moved to the Houston Aeros in 1977-78 for one season and played both his, and the league's, seventh and final WHA season in 1978-79 with the New England Whalers. He retired from hockey mid-way through the 1979-80 season, after returning to the NHL for the first time since 1971-72 as a member of the Hartford Whalers. Lacroix led the WHA in scoring in both 1972-73 (50-74—124) and 1974-75 (41-106—147), and had 100 or more scoring points in every season but his last.

14 The Avco World Cup was presented to the WHA's play-off champions each spring from 1973 to 1979. The final winner was the Winnipeg Jets, who captured the trophy in three of those seven seasons. With the absorption of the WHA into the NHL in 1979, the World Cup was left in the hands of the Jets, who installed it on a little shelf in the **Three Star Lounge** in the basement of the **Winnipeg Arena.** The lounge is used by the wives and friends of the Jets' players and management. It was later moved to the Director's Lounge in the Arena, where it remains on display today.

15 The WHA rules were similar to those used by the NHL and most other professional leagues. Here is how they differed when the league started:
A. **Tie Games:** In order to avoid as many tie games as possible, the WHA had a **ten-minute "sudden-death" overtime** period. [The NHL discontinued overtime during regular-season games during WWII (November 21, 1942) because of travel restrictions, and did not reinstitute it until the 1983-84 season, with a five-minute overtime.]

The WHA also experimented with a **shoot-out** during 1972 pre-season games similar to that used by some professional soccer leagues. Only one game came down to a shoot-out (which followed a scoreless overtime), when the Houston Aeros defeated the Minnesota Fighting Saints, 7-6, in Duluth, MN, on October 6, 1972. The score was 4-4 at the end of regulation time and the overtime frame was, of course, scoreless. Minnesota's Jimmy Johnson and Ted Hampson matched shoot-out goals by Houston's Larry Lund and Murray Hall before Don Grierson broke the deadlock for the Aeros. The WHA Board of Governors voted 9-2 against using the shoot-out in regular season play after the brief experiment.

B. **The Puck:** After experimenting with a fire-engine **red** puck, the WHA decided on a puck colored **deep blue** for its first season. "We haven't given up on red yet," said WHA President Gary Davidson as the season opened. "We're still working on it." The league went back to the standard **black** puck about half-way through the first season.

C. **Icing:** The puck could not be iced by a shorthanded team from inside their defending zone. If it were, the linesmen stopped play and faced-off the puck in the shorthanded team's zone. The puck could be iced by a team killing a penalty from outside their blueline without an icing call, however. Icing calls at even strength were the same in both the NHL and WHA.

D. **Altercations:** The WHA's rule covering the "third man" in a fight provided that he receive only a ten-minute misconduct penalty, as opposed to the NHL, which gives him a game misconduct. (WHA players were ejected if they were third man in a fight a second time in the same game.) "We're not promoting fighting," said WHA Referee-in-Chief Vern Buffey, "we just want to keep our stars on the ice so our fans can see them." Oh.

E. **Sticks:** In what could be called the "Bobby Hull Rule," the WHA permitted sticks to carry a **one-and-one-quarter inch curve.** In the NHL, the curve is limited to one-half inch. This rule was loved by shooters such as Hull. WHA goalies were less enthusiastic.

16 From 1967 to 1971, **Howard Baldwin** served as the ticket manager of the expansion NHL Flyers. He left the club in 1971 to found the New England Whalers and later became president of the WHA while continuing as the Whalers' managing general partner. He helped negotiate the absorption of the WHA into the NHL and remained with the new Hartford Whalers when they joined the NHL. The WHA's award for coach of the year was called the Howard Baldwin Award when first awarded to Whalers' coach Jack Kelley in 1973. It was later renamed the Robert Schmertz Memorial Trophy in honor of the Whalers' original board chairman.

17 **Gary L. Davidson,** who along with Dennis Murphy founded both the WHA and the ABA, was the league's first chief executive. The Gary L.

Davidson Trophy was the circuit's award for its Most Valuable Player, and it was awarded to Winnipeg's **Bobby Hull** for the 1972-73 season. The following year it was won by Houston's **Gordie Howe,** for whom the trophy was also renamed.

18 The WHA's penalty minute champ was also well known to NHL referees in the years after World Hockey went out of business. He was defenseman **Paul Baxter**, who compiled **962** minutes in just 290 WHA games with Cleveland (1975-76) and Quebec (1976-79). He came to the NHL with the Quebec Nordiques (1979-80) and then played the next three seasons with the **Pittsburgh Penguins,** with whom he compiled 409 minutes in 1981-82. That total not only led the NHL that season, it was second only to the 472 minutes assessed against Philadelphia's Dave Schultz in 1974-75 for a single-season total in the NHL. (Schultz also had 405 with Pittsburgh in 1977-78.) Baxter then moved on to the **Calgary Flames** for the 1983-84 season. A close second to Baxter on the all-time WHA list was defenseman Kim Clackson, who compiled 932 minutes in 271 games over four seasons with Indianapolis and Winnipeg, followed by Cam Connor with 904 in 274 games with Phoenix and Houston.

19 The WHA's eight original referees were: **Bill Friday** (senior referee), **Bob Sloan, Ron Ego, Brent Casselman, Willie Papp, Ray Thomas, Ron Asselstine,** and **Pierre Belanger.** Friday, Sloan, Ego, and Casselman all worked as NHL officials before their WHA service. **Asselstine** is the only original WHA official to work in the NHL later. He is currently an NHL linesman.

20 The twelve original WHA coaches were:

> **Ray Kinasewich** (Alberta Oilers)
> **Marcel Pronovost** (Chicago Cougars)
> **Bill Needham** (Cleveland Crusaders)
> **Bill Dineen** (Houston Aeros)
> **Terry Slater** (Los Angeles Sharks)
> **Glen Sonmor** (Minnesota Fighting Saints)
> **Jack Kelley** (New England Whalers)
> **Camille Henry** (New York Raiders)
> **Billy Harris** (Ottawa Nationals)
> **John McKenzie** (Philadelphia Blazers)
> **Maurice Filion** (Quebec Nordiques)
> **Bobby Hull** (Winnipeg Jets)

MYSTERY PLAYER I

SUPER QUESTION SIX: "DO YOU RECALL . . . THE WHA'S FIRST ALL-STARS?"

U nlike the NHL, which traditionally selects two All-Star Teams at the end of each season, the fledgling World Hockey Association decided to name three All-Star Teams at the end of its inaugural season, 1972-73. Each team consisted of six players (goaler, two defensemen, left wing, center and right wing) for a total of eighteen All-Stars. Our challenge to you in this sixth Super Question is to name all eighteen players in the WHA's First, Second, and Third 1972-73 All-Star Teams.

THE CLUE

To help you, we offer a clue to the identity of each player—an item of information about the hockey career of each man.

1972-73 WHA FIRST ALL-STAR TEAM

Goaler: After four busy WHA seasons, this great "money" goalie returned to play for the NHL club where he had made his name and later became the club's head coach.

Defense: 1. Twice an NHL All-Star, he was originally drafted by the WHA Los Angeles Sharks but was traded to Quebec before the season started.

2. Finished his playing careeer as captain of the Minnesota North Stars after the demise of the WHA.

Left-Wing: An eleven-time NHL All-Star, his defection to the WHA was the single most important factor in giving the new league credibility.

Center: Before playing for the WHA Philadelphia Blazers, he broke into the NHL across town with the Flyers. When the WHA folded in 1979, he closed the circuit's record book as its all-time leading scorer.

Right Wing: After scoring just ten goals the previous season (1971-72) in 78 games with the Buffalo Sabres, he led the WHA with 61 in 1972-73.

1972-73 WHA SECOND ALL-STAR TEAM

Goaler: A sure-fire Hall of Famer, he wore the unusual number "00" in the WHA and later won the Conn Smythe and Vezina twice in consecutive seasons without leaving town.

Defense: 1. As a rookie with Toronto, he set a then-NHL record of eight penalties and 48 minutes in a game—in his second week in the league.

2. Once traded for Sheldon Kannegeiser, his only NHL experience was 48 games with the St. Louis Blues.

Left Wing: Originally drafted by Alberta (Edmonton), he played 341 NHL games with Detroit, Oakland, and Toronto.

Center: Originally a defenseman, he was the only WHA player to score five goals in a game in that first season.

Right Wing: Once a 30-goal scorer with the Detroit Red Wings, he much later coached the AHL Adirondack Red Wings to a Calder Cup championship.

1972-73 WHA THIRD ALL-STAR TEAM

Goaler: Played six seasons in the WHA, all with New England, with a two year hiatus in the NHL with Buffalo, during which he played just 21 games. He also played in five other NHL cities during his career before he retired in 1981 from the Colorado Rockies.

Defense: 1. Originally a Toronto Maple Leaf, he later served the Whalers in the NHL as an assistant coach.

2. The first Whaler captain, this long-time Bruin missed an entire season when almost fatally injured in a pre-season stick fight. He later returned to the NHL as an assistant coach.

Left Wing: Nicknamed "Swoop" when in the NHL (Toronto, Boston, and California), he later became captain of the Toronto Toros.

Center: One of three brothers who played in the NHL, he once served as captain of the Montreal Jr. Canadiens. One of his other brothers also played in the WHA.

Right Wing: Scored 97 goals in his WHA career and one in the NHL.

MYSTERY PLAYER   J

THE ANSWERS

	FIRST TEAM	SECOND TEAM	THIRD TEAM
GOALER:	Gerry Cheevers	Bernie Parent	Al Smith
DEFENSE:	J.C. Tremblay	Jim Dorey	Rick Ley
	Paul Shmyr	Larry Hornung	Ted Green
LEFT WING:	Bobby Hull	Gary Jarrett	Wayne Carleton
CENTER:	Andre Lacroix	Ron Ward	Chris Bordeleau
RIGHT WING:	Danny Lawson	Tom Webster	Norm Beaudin

MYSTERY PLAYER K

PART VII

"DAD, WHY ARE THEY CALLED 'TARGETS'?" ... GOALIES

Goalies are called many things. Some call them "targets" because they make their living literally by standing in the line of fire. Others call them "pipe-polishers" or "twine-minders" because of the goal they must guard almost with their lives. But whatever you call them, they are different from other hockey players. Their lot in life is a lonely one, and they prefer it that way. A goalie is happiest when the other nine players on the ice for both teams are at the far end of the rink, because that means that he cannot be scored on—for another few seconds, anyway.

It takes a special breed of man to play goal in hockey. Unlike the hitter in baseball, who is a hero if he averages three hits for every ten tries, the goalie can make nine great saves and be the goat for missing the tenth. It is a position that has produced many great characters over the years, and many thrills for hockey's fans. Each of the questions on the following few pages relate to those masked men wearing, like the catcher in baseball, the "tools of ignorance."

1 Goalie Jim Craig of the 1980 Gold Medal-winning U.S. Olympic Team went on to play in the NHL with Atlanta and Boston in the two years immediately after the XIII Winter Olympic Games. What connection with major league hockey have the goalies with the two previous Olympic medal-winning U.S. teams had?

2 Two NHL teams which have always had a tradition of excellent goaltending are the Philadelphia Flyers and Montreal Canadiens. The Habs certainly proved that to the Flyers during the 1968-69 season when they shut them out (3-0, 1-0 and 4-0) in consecutive meetings— using three different goalies. Who were those three Montreal netminders, who are all sure-shots to make the Hockey Hall of Fame?

3 Who were the twelve original goalies claimed by the six new NHL clubs in the 1967 Expansion Draft, and which ones were also original-roster players in the WHA five years later?

4 During the 1968-69 season, the St. Louis Blues got their only win in Madison Square Garden in their first twelve years in the league by

MYSTERY PLAYER   L

defeating the New York Rangers. To earn that win, which proved to be so rare, the Blues needed not one but *three* goalies that night. Two of them have since been elected to the Hall of Fame. The third played just three minutes in the game and it proved to be the only action he would ever see in the NHL. He would eventually go on to make his name in another league and played through the 1981-82 season with the same team he had been with since 1970. Who were those goalies that the Blues used to defeat the Rangers that night?

5 Very few goalies ever get to play in a professional play-off final series and even fewer win one in their careers. In 1976, however, one goalie played not only in one professional play-off final, but in three. And he was the winning goalie in two championship games in a period of less than two weeks! Who was this goalie, with what three finalists did he play, and what championships did he help win?

6 The job of the goalie, obviously, is to prevent goals from being scored by the opposition. But twice in professional hockey history, a goalies have been credited with *scoring* a goal. Who were they and how did they score?

7 Some nights a player just has a goalie's "number" and sometimes that number is as high as five. Only once in NHL history have three individual players notched five-goal games against a single team (and goalie) in one season. Who was the goalie, what was his team, and who were the three single-game five-goal scorers?

8 What "grand experiment" was first attempted by goalie Clint Benedict of the Montreal Maroons in 1929?

9 A goalie who appears in sixty of his team's eighty games during an NHL season today is considered a workhorse. But until the mid-1960's, it was the norm for one goalie to play all his team's games every year. Who holds the virtually unbreakable "iron man" record for goalies in the NHL, how many consecutive games did he play, and how did his streak come to an end?

10 Montreal Canadien Hall of Fame goalie Ken Dryden won the Calder Memorial Trophy in 1971-72 as the NHL Rookie of the Year. What was unique about his winning the trophy that year?

11 On November 17, 1982, the Adirondack Red Wings defeated the Maine Mariners, 6-4, on their home ice at the Glens Falls Civic Center. While the result of the game was not historic, the hat trick that Mariner winger Mel Hewitt scored that night was. Why?

GOALIES . . . ANSWERS

1 Before the 1980 Gold Medal-winning performance at Lake Placid, the United States won medals seven previous times. In 1924, 1932, 1952, and 1956 the United States captured Silver Medals, and in 1936 they took the Bronze. The last two times the U.S. won medals before 1980 came in 1960 and 1972.

The 1960 U.S. team won the Gold Medal at Squaw Valley, CA. Their goalie was **Jack McCarten,** who had first been cut from the team but was asked to return at the insistance of the other players. (He did, but refused to wear either of the regular numbers for goalies, 1, or 30, but wore number 2 instead.) After leading the U.S. team to the Gold by beating the defending Olympic champion (1956) Soviets, 3-2, and the reigning (1959) World Champion Canadians, 2-1, McCarten was signed by the **New York Rangers.** After an impressive debut with the Broadway Blueshirts (1.75 goals-against average in four starts after joining the team late in the 1959-60 season), McCarten appeared in just eight more games with the Rangers the next year (4.91). That was his final NHL action, and he spent the next eleven years in the minor pro leagues until the advent of the WHA in 1972. He returned to his native St. Paul, MN, to play for the WHA **Minnesota Fighting Saints** from 1972 to 1975. Ironically the Saints' other goalie (1972-77) was another Olympic medalist, **Mike Curran,** who had just won a Silver Medal with the U.S. team at the Winter Olympic games in Sapporo, Japan.

2 Two of the goalies should be easy, as they made much of their fame playing for the Habs. They were **Lorne "Gump" Worsley** and **Rogie Vachon.** Worsley shut out the Flyers, 3-0, at the Montreal Forum on November 21, 1968, by stopping all 22 Philadelphia shots, while Bobby Rousseau, John Ferguson, and Gilles Tremblay each put one of the Habs' 49 past Bernie Parent. Vachon got his whitewash on January 16, 1969, at the Spectrum in Philadelphia (25 saves) as Montreal won, 4-0, on goals by Rousseau (a pair), Ferguson, and Yvan Cournoyer in 40 shots on Parent. The third Canadian goalie who shut out the Flyers was none other than future Hall of Famer **Tony Esposito,** who appeared in just thirteen career games with the Habs (all in 1968-69) before being claimed in the June, 1969, reverse draft by the Chicago Black Hawks. He shut out the Flyers, 1-0, on December 14, 1968, making 25 stops while Ferguson, again, beat Parent, who stopped 46 of 47 Montreal shots that night at the Forum.

3 The twelve original goalies taken in the 1967 Expansion Draft (and the teams they were drafted from) were:
LOS ANGELES: **Terry Sawchuck** (Toronto), **Wayne Rutledge** (New York Rangers)
CALIFORNIA: **Charlie Hodge** (Montreal), **Gary Smith** (Toronto)
PITTSBURGH: **Joe Daley** (Detroit), **Roy Edwards** (Chicago)

MYSTERY PLAYER M

MINNESOTA: **Cesare Maniago** (New York Rangers), **Garry Baumen** (Montreal)
PHILADELPHIA: **Bernie Parent** (Boston), **Doug Favell** (Boston)
ST. LOUIS: **Glenn Hall** (Chicago), **Don Caley** (Detroit)

Three of those twelve original expansion goalies were on WHA rosters when that league started play in 1972. They were: **Bernie Parent** (Philadelphia Blazers), **Wayne Rutledge** (Houston Aeros), and **Joe Daley** (Winnipeg Jets).

4 **Jacques Plante** and **Glenn Hall** were the Hall of Fame goalies who were the Blues regular netminders for the 1968-69 season. That particular night, Hall started the game while Plante was given the night off and was sitting in the stands. As Hall's back-up, Scotty Bowman had dressed a 22-year-old rookie named **Robbie Irons.** Hall was ejected during the game and was forced to retire to the sidelines. Irons entered the game while Plante headed for the dressing room to put on his equipment. After three minutes of play, Irons was "hurt" and was replaced by Plante, who finished the game for the Blues. Irons played two seasons for the CHL Kansas City Blues before joining the IHL **Fort Wayne Komets,** with whom he played until 1982.

5 The Spring of 1976 was something special for goalie **Gaye Cooley.** The former Michigan State University netminder was in goal for the SHL **Charlotte Checkers** when that club won the Southern League's play-off championship. [Cooley was with Charlotte for four seasons (1971-72; 1973-76).] He then joined the NAHL **Philadelphia Firebirds** as they were in the semi-finals of their play-offs. (Firebird goalie Rejean Lemelin had been injured earlier and was out for the remainder of the play-offs.) The Firebirds defeated the defending Lockhart Cup champion Johnstown Jets with Cooley in goal in a "classic" 14-10 series-clinching game and went on to upset the regular-season champion Beauce Jaros to win the play-off crown. It was Cooley's second in two weeks. He then joined the WHA **New England Whalers** and made one brief appearance for them in the "USA Finals," during which the Whalers were defeated by the Houston Aeros, four games to three. (Houston was defeated in the Avco World Cup finals by the Winnipeg Jets, four games to none.)

6 The first professional goalie to be credited with a goal scored was **Michel Plasse,** who was then playing for the CHL Kansas City Blues. In a game played at Kansas City against the Oklahoma City Blazers on February 21, 1971, the Blues were holding a slim 3-2 lead late in the game as the Blazers were given a power play. Oklahoma City pulled goalie John Adams for an extra attacker and were swarming around Plasse when the puck came to the Kansas City goalie. He fired the puck the length of the ice, knowing that no icing would be called with his team short-handed. The puck found its way into the net at the other end and Plasse became the first goalie to score a goal in professional hockey

history. Unfortunately, a severe snowstorm that night kept the crowd at less than 600 people to witness that bit of history.

The second goaler to be credited with a goal was **Billy Smith** of the New York Islanders. On the night of November 28, 1979, Smith was in goal for the Isles, who were playing the Colorado Rockies at McNichols Arena in Denver, CO. With the Rockies in possession of the puck, a delayed penalty was signaled against the Islanders, and Colorado goalie Bill MacKenzie skated to the bench for an extra attacker. The Rockies took a shot on goal which deflected into the corner off of Smith's stick, making him the last Islander to touch (but not *control*) the puck. The Rockies' Randy Pierce reached the puck first and passed it out to Rob Ramage at the blueline, but Ramage missed the pass and it went the length of the ice and ended up in the back of the Colorado net. As Smith was the last Islander to touch the puck before it entered the Colorado net, he was credited with the goal.

7 The **Phildelphia Flyers** and goalie **Pete Peeters** were the victim of three individual five-goal games during the 1981-82 season. The first player to solve the Flyers for five was Edmonton's **Wayne Gretzky,** who scored his 46th through 50th goals of the season on December 30, 1981, at the Northlands Coliseum in Edmonton. That gave Gretzky the record for the fastest fifty goals from the start of the season (his 39th game), breaking by eleven games the record held by Maurice Richard and Mike Bossy of fifty goals in fifty games. (It should be noted that Peeters only let in four of them. The fifth goal was into an empty net.) On February 13, 1982, the Islanders' **Bryan Trottier** scored goals one each of his five shots on Pete that night at the Nassau Coliseum. Three weeks later, on March 2, 1982, Peeters was again dented for five by Winnipeg's **Willy Lindstrom** at the Spectrum in Philadelphia.

8 Clint Benedict, the great goalie for the Ottawa Senators and Montreal Maroons, was the first to experiment with a **mask** in hockey. Benedict had already won four Stanley Cups (three with Ottawa, one with Montreal) when he first tried a cumbersome leather mask during the 1929-30 season, his seventeenth since he started playing senior hockey as a 17-year-old. Benedict's nose was shattered by a shot from the stick of the Canadiens' Howie Morenz that season, which sidelined him for a month. Benedict then tried the mask in a game against the Chicago Black Hawks, which he lost, 2-1. That was enough for him and he discarded the mask, blaming it for the loss. Benedict's career was ended later that season when he was again hit by a shot by Morenz, this time in the throat. (He was elected to the Hall of Fame in 1965.) Jacques Plante reintroduced the mask almost thirty years later when, on November 1, 1959, he was gashed across his cheek and nose by a shot by the Rangers' Andy Bathgate at Madison Square Garden. After repairs he returned to the ice wearing the mask, which has since become a standard piece of every goalie's equipment.

MYSTERY PLAYER N

9 The great **Glenn Hall** holds the undisputed record for consecutive games for a goalie at 502, established between opening night of his rookie season with the Detroit Red Wings (1955-56) and November 7, 1962, his fifth season with the Chicago Black Hawks. Hall had not missed a regular season or play-off game in over six seasons, and if you count those post-season appearances (the NHL does not), his consecutive streak was actually ended at 551. At practice the day before his streak ended, Hall strained his back as he tried to break in a new pair of pads. After a fitful night, he skated the warmup and knew that his streak was in danger. When Boston's Murray Oliver beat him easily with a fifteen-footer that he would normally have stopped in his sleep, he skated to the Chicago bench and then left the ice, ending his streak at 33,135 minutes and thirty-three seconds at the 10:20 mark of the first period. He was replaced in goal by Denis DeJordy.

10 When **Ken Dryden** won the Calder Memorial Trophy for the 1971-72 season he became the first—and so far only—player to win the Rookie of the Year *award* after winning another major NHL trophy. Dryden spent most of the 1970-71 season playing for the AHL Montreal Voyageurs. Late in the season he was called up to the parent Canadiens and appeared in six games, in which he compiled a sparkling 1.65 goals-against average. He continued to get the call in the play-offs that spring and led the Habs to a Stanley Cup championship while playing all twenty games and winning the Conn Smythe Trophy as play-off MVP. Since he had not yet played in twenty-five regular season games, he was still considered a "rookie" the following season.

11 Hewitt's three-goal **hat trick** that night was scored against **three different goalies.** Veteran **Gilles Gilbert** started the game for Adirondack and surrendered his goal to Hewitt just twenty-four seconds into the game. He was replaced by backup **Claude Legris** at the 13:39 mark of the first period, when he retired from the game because of injury. At 14:13 of the second period, Hewitt scored his second goal of the game, this time against Legris. In the meantime, **Jimmy Rutherford,** another long-time NHL veteran then on assignment to Adirondack, had come out of the stands to dress as back-up in case of emergency and was sitting on the bench.

At the 10:43 mark of the third period, a brawl broke out in which Legris became involved and for which referee Dan Cournoyer assessed him a game misconduct penalty. Rutherford was now forced to take over, and just under eight minutes later Hewitt completed his hat trick with a goal at 18:36—his third goal of the game against the third different goalie.

SUPER QUESTION SEVEN: HOCKEY'S MOST EXCLUSIVE TEAM . . . THE NHL's RETIRED NUMBERS

Thousands of players have performed on the ice in the NHL since it was first organized in 1917. Each has been assigned one or more numbers to wear during his NHL career. But in the league's first 67 years of operation just 30 of those numbers have been retired to honor players who wore them. Some numbers were retired when their owners met an untimely death from accident while on the teams. Most have been permanently set aside to honor the great careers of the man who made them famous.

For our seventh Super Question for you, we ask you to name the players, their teams, and the number that was retired in each man's honor. To help you, we supply you with two clues. The first is a list of all the actual numbers that have been returned and the number of clubs that have retired each. For the second we name the clubs that have retired numbers and the number of sweaters each has honored with retirement.

THE FIRST CLUE

We list below the actual numbers that have been retired by currently active NHL clubs, and the number of teams that have retired each sweater.

SWEATER NUMBER	RETIRING TEAMS
# 1	one
# 2	three
# 3	four
# 4	three
# 5	two
# 6	one
# 7	three
# 8	one
# 9	five
#11	one
#15	one
#16	one
#19	two
#21	two

THE SECOND CLUE

Now that you know the actual numbers that have been retired and the number of teams that have retired each, we will give you the names of the sixteen current NHL franchises that have retired player sweaters and the number of jerseys retired by each.

RETIRING TEAM	SWEATERS RETIRED
Boston Bruins	six
Bufflo Sabres	one
Chicago Black Hawks	two
Detroit Red Wings	two
Edmonton Oilers	one
Hartford Whalers	three
Minnesota North Stars	one
Montreal Canadiens	four
New York Rangers	one
Philadelphia Flyers	two
Pittsburgh Penguins	one
Quebec Nordiques	one
St. Louis Blues	two
Toronto Maple Leafs	one
Vancouver	one
Washington Capitals	one

MYSTERY PLAYER O

MYSTERY PLAYER P

MYSTERY PLAYER Q

THE ANSWERS

Here is the list (by teams) of the 30 retired sweater numbers in the NHL, the players who were honored, and the years each man played for his club.

BOSTON BRUINS	# 2	**Eddie Shore** (1926-40)
	# 3	**Lionel Hitchman** (1925-34)
	# 4	**Bobby Orr** (1966-76)
	# 5*	**Dit Clapper** (1927-47)
	# 9	**Johnny Bucyk** (1957-78)
	#15	**Milt Schmidt** (1936-55)
BUFFALO SABRES	# 2	**Tim Horton** (1972-74) [Killed in a car accident]
CHICAGO BLACK HAWKS	# 9	**Bobby Hull** (1957-72)
	#21	**Stan Mikita** (1958-80)
DETROIT RED WINGS	# 6	**Larry Aurie** (1927-39)
	# 9	**Gordie Howe** (1946-71) [See also Hartford]
EDMONTON OILERS	# 3	**Al Hamilton** (1972-80) [1972-79 in WHA]
HARTFORD WHALERS	# 2	**Rick Ley** (1972-81)
	# 9	**Gordie Howe** (1977-80) [1977-79 in WHA]
	#19	**Johnny McKenzie** (1976-79) [All in WHA]
MINNESOTA NORTH STARS	#19	**Bill Masterton** (1967-68) [Killed in on-ice game accident]
MONTREAL CANADIENS	# 4	**Jean Beliveau** (1950-71)
	# 7	**Howie Morenz** (1923-37) [Died after surgery for broken leg]
	# 9	**Maurice Richard** (1942-60)
	#16	**Henri Richard** (1955-75) [Only retired-number brothers]
NEW YORK RANGERS	# 7	**Rod Gilbert** (1960-78)
PHILADELPHIA FLYERS	# 1	**Bernie Parent** (1967-71; 73-79) [Eye injury ended career]
	# 4	**Barry Ashbee** (1970-74) [Died of leukemia while a coach]
PITTSBURGH PENGUINS	#21	**Michel Briere** (1969-70) [Killed in car accident]
QUEBEC NORDIQUES	# 3	**J.C. Tremblay** (1972-79) [All in WHA]

ST. LOUIS BLUES # 3 **Bob Gassoff** (1973-77)
[Killed in motorcycle accident]
8 **Barclay Plager** (1967-1977)

TORONTO MAPLE LEAFS # 5 **Bill Barilko** (1946-51)
[Killed in off-season plane crash]

VANCOUVER CANUCKS #11 **Wayne Maki** (1971-73)
[Died of brain tumor]

WASHINGTON CAPITALS # 7 **Yvon Labre** (1974-81)

*The Bruins "unretired" Dit Clapper's #5 at the start of the 1983-84 season to give it to defenseman Guy Lapointe, who had worn that number for many years with the Canadiens. After considerable objection from the hockey community, Clapper's number was again retired and Lapointe was assigned #27.

PART VIII

"AND THE WINNER IS. . ."
. . . .HOCKEY TROPHIES

I n hockey that pot at the end of the rainbow is not gold (that comes when the player signs his contract), but silver. It may be called the Stanley Cup, the Adams Cup, the Calder Cup, or the Turner Cup. And there are many individual and team awards to recognize achievements other than play-off championships. The questions we pose on the next few pages all relate to those "silver pots" which are so highly prized in hockey.

1 We start you off with the names of twenty-six hockey trophies, awards, and plaques which either have been or are still awarded every year in the leagues of professional or amateur hockey in North America. What accomplishments do each of these recognize?

A. Adams Cup	N. Hunt Memorial Trophy
B. Adams Award	O. Turner Cup
C. Sollenberger Trophy	P. Memorial Cup
D. Mitchell Cup	Q. Hobey Baker Award
E. Ivan Trophy	R. Cunningham Plaque
F. Patrick Cup	S. Conn Smythe Trophy
G. Garret Memorial Trophy	T. Stafford Smythe Trophy
H. Centennial Cup	U. Leader Cup
I. Orr Trophy	V. Lockhart Cup
J. Jennings Trophy	W. Longman Memorial Trophy
K. Calder Cup	X. Air Canada Cup
L. Calder Memorial Trophy	Y. Powers Memorial Trophy
M. Esposito Trophy	Z. Shore Plaque

2 Until 1982, the Vezina Trophy was awarded to the goalies (minimum 25 games played) on the team that allowed the fewest goals-against during each NHL season. What coach has guided the most different teams to Vezina Trophy-winning seasons, what teams were they, and what season(s) did each win the Vezina under this coach?

3 Championships usually bring with them the promise of future success and recognition, but not always. What unusual fate did each of the following professional teams suffer in the season after winning both the regular season and play-off championships in their leagues? Here are

the teams: 1964-65 St. Paul Rangers (CHL), 1969-70 Buffalo Bisons (AHL), 1981-82 New Brunswick Hawks (AHL), 1969-70 Vancouver Canucks (WHL), 1966-67 Pittsburgh Hornets (AHL).

4 Many players have been repeat winners of the same NHL trophy, but only six men have won the same trophy with two different teams. Who are these six players, what were the awards they won, and with what two different teams did each capture their trophies?

5 Which NHL players have won each of the following major trophies in three or more consecutive seasons, and who broke each man's hold on each award?

A. The Hart Memorial Trophy
B. The Arthur H. Ross Trophy
C. The Georges Vezina Trophy
D. The James Norris Memorial Trophy
E. The Lady Byng Memorial Trophy
F. The Frank J. Selke Trophy

6 The awarding of the Memorial Cup in 1983 was different from all previous presentations of the award in two ways. What were they?

7 For what was each of the following WHA trophies awarded, and who was the first winner of each?

A. The W.D. (Bill) Hunter Trophy
B. The Ben Hatskin Trophy
C. The Paul Deneau Award
D. The Lou Kaplan Award
E. The Dennis A. Murphy Award

8 Many NHL clubs present annual awards to their players at the end of each season. What NHL club presents each of the following awards, and what does each prize recognize?

A. The Ashbee Trophy
B. The Elizabeth C. Dufresne Trophy
C. Stu Evans Trophy
D. James G. Balmer Award
E. Wayne Larkin Memorial Trophy
F. The Michel Briere Memorial Trophy
G. Frank Boucher Trophy
H. Frank Keyes Memorial Award
I. West Side Association Trophy
J. Bill Masterson Memorial Cup

9 The Molson Cup is presented each year to the player on each of six of the seven Canadian-based NHL teams who has the most points for "Three Star" selections. Which is the only Canadian-based club without a Molson Cup and why don't they have one?

10 Which NHL teams have won each of the following major NHL awards the greatest number of times?

A. Art Ross Trophy
B. Hart Trophy
C. Lady Byng Trophy
D. Vezina Trophy
E. Calder Trophy
F. James Norris Trophy

11 Only twice in NHL history has a player won both the Calder Trophy and another major NHL award in the same year. Who were they, and what other trophy did each win?

MYSTERY PLAYER R

MYSTERY PLAYER S

HOCKEY TROPHIES . . . ANSWERS

1 Here is what each of our twenty-six hockey trophies, awards, and plaques recognize:

A. **CHL Play-off Championship.** Named for Jack Adams, CHL President (1963-68)

B. **NHL Coach of the Year.** Also named for Jack Adams (above), GM/Coach, Detroit Red Wings (1927-63)

C. **AHL Scoring Championship.** Named for John B. Sollenberger, AHL Board Chairman and President, Hershey Bears

D. **ACHL Play-off Championship.** Named for Johnny Mitchell, long-time manager of the Johnstown Jets.

E. **CHL Regular Season MVP.** Named for Tommy Ivan, GM, Chicago Black Hawks, and coach, Detroit Red Wings.

F. **WHL Play-off Championship.** Named for Lester Patrick, builder, player, GM and coach, New York Rangers

G. **AHL Rookie of the Year.** Named for Dudley "Red" Garret, AHL player killed in WWII while in service with the Royal Canadian Navy

H. **Tier II Canadian Junior Championship.**

I. **CHL Defenseman of the Year.** Named for Robert G. (Bobby) Orr, top scoring defenseman in NHL history with Boston Bruins, and Chicago Black Hawks

J. **Top NHL Defensive Team** [Awarded to goalie(s)]. Named for William Jennings, President, New York Rangers

K. **AHL Play-off Championship.** Named for Frank Calder, first President, NHL

L. **NHL Rookie of the Year.** Also named for Frank Calder

M. **CHL Scoring Championship.** Named for Phil Esposito, NHL's second all-time leading scorer with Chicago Black Hawks, Boston Bruins, and New York Rangers

N. **AHL Sportsmanship, Dedication and Determination.** Named for Fred T. Hunt, GM/Coach, Buffalo Bisons

O. **IHL Play-off Championship.** Named for Joseph Turner, Windsor, ON., amateur goalie killed in WWII

P. **Canadian Major Junior Play-off Championship.**

Q. **NCAA College Hockey Player of the Year.** Named for Hobey Baker, player at Princeton University (1910-14) [Elected to Hockey Hall of Fame, 1945].

R. **AHL Regular Season MVP.** Named for Les Cunningham, high-scoring player with the Cleveland Barons for ten years.

S. **NHL Play-off MVP.** Named for Conn Smythe, owner, Manager, and Coach, Toronto Maple Leafs

T. **Memorial Cup Play-off MVP,** Named for Stafford Smythe, son of Conn Smythe and owner, Toronto Maple Leafs

U. **WHL Regular Season MVP.** Named for George Leader, first president, WHL

V. **NAHL. Play-off Championship.** Named for Thomas Lockhart, President, New York Rovers, and long-time commissioner, EHL

W. **IHL Rookie of the Year.** Named for Garry F. Longman, IHL player killed in an accident after his rookie year.

X. **Canadian Midget Play-off Championship.** Named for Air Canada, tournament sponsor.

Y. **OHL Scoring Championship.** Named for Eddie Powers

Z. **AHL Defenseman of the Year.** Named for Eddie Shore, legendary Hall of Fame defenseman for the Boston Bruins, long-time owner of the Springfield Indians

2 **William Scott "Scotty" Bowman** has coached three different franchises to Vezina Trophy-winning seasons, winning the award a total of seven times. Bowman's top defensive clubs were:

1— **St. Louis Blues** (1968-69)

2— **Montreal Canadiens** (1972-73, 1975-76, 1976-77, 1977-78, 1978-79)

3— **Buffalo Sabres** (1979-80)

3 Each of these five teams folded after winning championships. Pittsburgh, Vancouver, and Buffalo all ceased operations to allow new NHL clubs to take their places. New Brunswick was operated jointly by the Toronto Maple Leafs and Chicago Black Hawks. The team was disbanded when Toronto (who owned the franchise) decided to move it to St. Catherines, Ontario, for the 1982-83 season and operate the team alone as the St. Catherines Saints. Chicago sent their players to the Springfield Indians for the 1982-83 season. The Edmonton Oilers moved a new franchise into the Hawks' building and started operation in 1982-83 as the Moncton Alpines. The CHL St. Paul Rangers disbanded and were not replaced by another team until two years later, when the NHL Minnesota North Stars joined the league as an expansion franchise.

4 Here are the six NHL players who have won the same major individual award with two different teams:

1— **Clint Smith** won the Lady Byng with the New York Rangers (1939) and Chicago Black Hawks (1944)

2— **Leonard "Red" Kelly** won the Lady Byng with the Detroit Red Wings (1951-53-54) and Toronto Maple Leafs (1961)

3— **Jacques Plante** won the Vezina Trophy with the Montreal Canadiens (1956-57-58-59-60 and 62) and the St. Louis Blues (1969)

4— **Glenn Hall** won the Vezina Trophy with the Chicago Black Hawks (1963 and 67) and the St. Louis Blues (1969)

5— **Jean Retelle** won the Lady Byng with the New York Rangers (1972) and the Boston Bruins (1976)

6— **Marcel Dionne** won the Lady Byng with the Detroit Red Wings (1975) and the Los Angeles Kings (1977)

5 The following fourteen players have won one or more major individual NHL awards three or more consecutive times. (The player who broke each multiple award winner's streak is in brackets [ ].)

A. Hart Trophy

Bobby Orr (Boston) 1970-71-72
[Bob Clarke]
Wayne Gretzky (Edmonton) 1980-81-82-83

B. Ross Trophy

Gordie Howe (Detroit)
1951-52-53-54
[Bernie Geoffrion]
Phil Esposito (Boston) 1971-72-73-74
[Bobby Orr]
Guy Lafleur (Montreal) 1976-77-78
[Bryan Trottier]
Wayne Gretzky (Edmonton) 1981-82-83

C. Vezina Trophy

George Hainsworth (Montreal Canadiens)
1927-28-29
[Tiny Thompson]
Bill Durnan (Montreal) 1944-45-46-47
[Turk Broda]
Jacques Plante (Montreal) 1956-57-58-59-60
[Johnny Bower]
Ken Dryden (Montreal) 1976-77-78-79
and
Michel Laroeque (Montreal) 1977-78-79
[Bob Sauve & Don Edwards]

D. Norris Trophy

Doug Harvey (Montreal) 1955-56-57-58
[Tom Johnson]
Doug Harvey (Montreal) 1960-61-62
[Pierre Pilote]
Pierre Pilote (Chicago) 1963-34-35
[Jacques Laperriere]
Bobby Orr (Boston) 1968-69-70-71-72-73-74-75
[Larry Robinson]

E. Byng Trophy

Frank Boucher (New York Rangers)
1928-29-30-31
[Joe Primeau]
Frank Boucher (New York Rangers) 1933-34-35
[Doc Romnes]

F. Selke Trophy

Bob Gainey (Montreal) 1978-79-80-81
[Steve Kasper]

6 The 1983 Memorial Cup presentation was different from all previous awardings of the Canadian "Major Junior" play-off championship trophy in that the tournament (and therefore the presentation) took place in the **United States** (Portland, OR) for the first time, and it was won for the first time by a team based in the United States, the Portland Winter Hawks.

7 Here are the accomplishments recognized by each of the five WHA awards and the first winner of each (1973):

A. **Scoring Championship**—Andre Lacroix (Philadelphia Blazers)

B. **Best Goaltender**—Gerry Cheevers (Cleveland Crusaders)

C. **Most Sportsmanlike Player**—Ted Hampson (Minnesota Fighting Saints)

D. **Rookie of the Year**—Terry Caffrey (New England Whalers)

E. **Defenseman of the Year**—J.C. Tremblay (Quebec Nordiques)

8 Each award is presented by the club, a sponsor, or the booster club, for the following achievements:

A. **Philadelphia Flyers**—Best Defenseman

B. **Boston Bruins**—"Most outstanding player in home games"

C. **Detroit Red Wings**—Most sportsmanlike player

D. **Pittsburgh Penguins**—Individual contribution to hockey in Pittsburgh

E. **Buffalo Sabres**—Most Valuable Player voted by teammates

F. **Pittsburgh Penguins**—Rookie of the Year

G. **New York Rangers**—Ranger Fan Club's award

H. **Hartford Whalers**—Unsung Hero

I. **New York Rangers**—Most Valuable Player

J. **Minnesota North Stars**—Most Valuable Player voted by teammates

9 As the name implies, the **Molson Cup** is sponsored by the major Canadian brewer of beer and ale, Brasserie Molson. It is presented to one player each from Montreal, Toronto, Winnipeg, Calgary, Edmonton, and Vancouver at the end of each season to recognize earning the most poiints in "Three Star" selections in each club's home games. The only Canadian-based NHL club that does not have a Molson Cup is the **Quebec Nordiques,** and for a very good reason . The Nordiques are owned by Molson's biggest brewing competitor, Carling O'Keefe!

10 The NHL major individual awards play a major role in post-season public relations for the league, but they also serve as an indication as to why some teams dominate the league history with excellence. Here are the clubs that have been most often represented by the winners of six of the league's major awards. (Note: The Art Ross Trophy has only been awarded since 1948, but we will consider all the scoring champions from 1927 to 1982 as Ross winners for purposes of this answer.)

A. Ross Trophy 1) Montreal Canadiens—
(awarded 66 times) 16 winners
Tie - 2) Boston and Toronto—
11 times each

(Cont. Next Page)

B. Hart Trophy
   (awarded 60 times

1) Montreal Canadiens—
   15 winners
2) Boston Bruins—
   12 winners
3) Detroit Red Wings—
   8 winners

C. Byng Trophy
   (awarded 59 times)

1) New York Rangers—
   14 winners
2) Detroit Red Wings—
   10 winners
Tie - 3) Toronto and Chicago—
   8 winners each

D. Vezina Trophy
   (awarded 57 times)

1) Montreal Canadiens-
   24 winners
Tie - 2) Boston and Chicago—
   8 winners each
4) Toronto Maple Leafs—
   7 winners

E. Calder Trophy
   (awarded 52 times)

1) New York Rangers—
   9 winners
2) Toronto Maple Leafs—
   8 winners
Tie - 3) Boston, Chicago, Detroit &
   Montreal—
   6 winners

F. Norris Trophy
   (awarded 30 times)

1) Montreal Canadiens—
   10 winners
2) Boston Bruins —
   8 winners
3) Chicago Black Hawks—
   winners

11 In 1970, **Tony Esposito** of the Chicago Black Hawks won both the **Calder Memorial Trophy** as the league's top rookie and the **Vezina Trophy** for his outstanding performance in goal. Tony "O" appeared in 63 of the Hawks' 76 games as a 25-year-old rookie compiling a 2.17 goals-against average. His 15 shut-outs in 1969-70 not only led the league that year, it still stands as the most in any NHL season since 1919. Boston goalie **Frank Brimsak** also won both trophies in 1939.

SUPER QUESTION EIGHT: "WHAT DO NICK FOTIU. . .AND AL ARBOUR. . .HAVE IN COMMON?"

We have something a little different for you for our eighth Super Question. Here we are looking to test your knowledge of unusual relationships in hockey. Below we present you a series of lists which somehow relate to hockey. Each item on each list also has some unusual and particular relationship to the other items on the same list. Your job is to determine what that relationship is. Keep an open mind as you consider each group of related people, places, things, or whatever. And don't jump at the first thing you think of. Some of the relationships are subtle; some are so "obvious" that they may be easily missed.

Not all the items on each list necessarily are hockey related, and the peculiar relationship they share may also have something to do with the world outside of the hockey rink. After you have gone through the lists and given each some thought, you may turn to our list of clues for some help on the ones you haven't figured out yet.

This question is meant to be fun, so just let yourself go and enjoy it.

A. Hall of Fame members Sylvanius "Syl" Apps and Leonard "Red" Kelly
B. Madison Square Garden (34th St.), Maple Leaf Gardens, The Spectrum, and Le Colisee (Quebec City)
C. 1982-83 NHL Award winners Bob Clarke, Pete Peeters, Wayne Gretzky, Rod Langway, Roland Melanson, Billy Smith, and Steve Larmer
D. Baldy Northcott, Bob Kelly, Eddie Shack, Bobby Orr, Metro Prystai, Wayne Merrick, Gordie Howe, and Bill Barilko
E. Larry Zeidel, Murray Bannerman, and Mike Veisor
F. Robin Burns, Dave Christian, Lars Lindgren, Ken Linseman, Dave Michayluk, Jim Schoenfield, and Jim Hamilton
G. Philadelphia Flyer coaches Fred Shero and Bob McCammon
H. Philadelphia Flyer GM/coach Bob McCammon and former Philadelphia Phillies first baseman Pete Rose
I. Edmonton defenseman Randy Gregg and former major league pitcher George Medich
J. Pittsburgh Penguin GM Eddie Johnston, NHL linesman Kevin Collins, and current or past NHL players Paul Holmgren, Dave Hanson, Bruce Boudreau, Ralph MacSweyn, Jack Carlson, and his brother, Steve Carlson
K. NHL head or assistant coaches Ted Green, Bernie Parent, Gerry Cheevers, Larry Pleau, John Cunniff, Rick Ley, Bill Sutherland, and Nick Polano
L. Goalies Glenn Hall and Roger Crozier

M. Gordie Howe, Bobby Hull, Bobby Orr, Bob Clarke, Eddie Shore, Stan Mikita, Phil Esposito, Johnny Bucyk, Alex Delvecchio, Terry Sawchuk, and Charles M. Schulz

N. Clarence Campbell, Fran Huck, Ken Dryden, and Gerry Meehan.

O. Jack Adams, Tommy Ivan, Phil Esposito, Bobby Orr, Ken McKenzie, Don Ashby, Max McNab, Clarence Campbell, Terry Sawchuk, Jake Milford, and Bob Gassoff

P. Red Berenson, Jean Guy Talbot, Keith Allen, Larry Wilson, Billy Dea, Bart Crashley, Leo Boiven, Fred Glover, Johnny Bucyk, Bill Dineen, Al Arbour, Tom Webster, Bert Marshall, Floyd Smith, Doug Barkley, Murray Oliver, Parker MacDonald, Red Kelly, Ted Lindsay, Alex Delvecchio, Mark Howe, Dave Keon, Charlie Burns, Pit Martin, Andre Lacroix, Gerry Hart, Bernie Johnston, Andy Bathgate, Dale Rolfe, and Nick Fotiu

Q. Gump Worsley, Harry Lumley, Jacques Plante, Al Rollins, and Johnny Bower

R. Baz Bastien, Greg Neeld, Bill Chadwick, Glen Sonmor, and Bernie Parent

S. Rick Dudley, Doug Favell, and Barry Ashbee

T. Frank Mahovlich, Mike Nykoluk, and Darryl Sittler

U. Wayne Thomas, Mario Lessard, and Robbie Moore

V. Washington Capitals, Philadelphia Flyers, Chicago Black Hawks, Boston Bruins, Hartford Whalers, Los Angeles Kings, and New York Rangers

W. St. Paul Saints (IHL), St. Paul Rangers (CPHL), Buffalo Bisons (AHL), Omaha Knights (CHL), and Philadelphia Flyers (NHL)

X. Former NHL coaches Earl Ingerfield, Leo Boivin, Al MacNeil, Billy Dea, and Ken Schinkel

Y. Center Bobby Collyard and right wing Gordie Brooks

Z. Steve Witiuk, Bob Charlebois, Dennis Hextall, Derek Sanderson, Hank Nowak, Earl Anderson, Ron Low, Boris Fistric, Bob Girard, Paul MacKinnon, Randy Velischek, and Fred Boimstruck.

THE CLUES

Here is a clue about the unusual relationship of the items in each list. But be careful—some are a little tricky.

A. They were "the people's choice" in more ways than one.
B. A windstorm brought these four buildings together.
C. The Army may have never gotten around to them.
D. Each was the cause for drinking.
E. While each played for Chicago, their brotherhood goes deeper than that.
F. Some might think them unlucky.
G. IHL/AHL.
H. They are as close as two Philadelphia sports figures could be in one way.
I. Both provide their clubs with healing influences.
J. "SLAPSHOT" was of special interest to them.
K. Each had a new beginning in 1972.
L. Both "won" in defeat.
M. Each made his mark in the United States.
N. Each knows what it means to be brief.

O. Each brings honor to another once a year.
P. Each has accomplished the same thing from one to 210 times.
Q. None was dented less than 50 times.
R. Each had a special view of hockey.
S. Hockey was not their only game.
T. They are the only three to do this since 1927.
U. Each had a nothing debut.
V. They formed a special tribe of their own in a brief seven year span.
W. Each came out of the fog and into the bright sunshine of victory.
Y. They just couldn't get away from each other.
Z. Each brought the same return.

MYSTERY PLAYER T

THE ANSWERS

A. Both were elected to **Parliament** in Canada (MP's).

B. All four buildings were the venues of **home games** of the **Philadelphia Flyers** during the 1967-68 season. A windstorm in late February, 1968, blew off part of the roof of the Spectrum, forcing the Flyers to play both their home and away games "on the road" for the final month of the season.

C. **None** of these 1982-83 NHL Award winners was a first round draft pick. Selke winner Bob Clarke was taken in the 2nd-round in 1969; Vezina winner Peter Peeters was an 8th-round pick in 1977; Hart and Ross winner Wayne Gretzky was a member of the Edmonton Oilers which joined the NHL during his draft year so he was never drafted as an amateur; Norris winner Rod Langway was a 2nd-round pick in 1977; Jennings co-winner Rollie Melanson was a 3rd-round pick in 1979; teammate Bill Smith (Jennings and Smythe) was a 3rd-round pick in 1970; and Calder winner Steve Larmer was a 6th-round pick in 1980.

D. Each has scored a **Stanley Cup-winning** goal during his career.

E. All three were **Jewish** players in the NHL.

F. They are the only seven players to wear **#13** in the NHL since expansion. Burns was first (Kansas City Scouts, 1974), followed by Christian (Winnipeg Jets, 1980), Lindgren (Vancouver Canucks, 1981, after wearing #3 for his first three seasons with the club), Linseman (Edmonton Oilers, 1982), Michayluk (Philadelphia Flyers, 1982), Schoenfeld (Boston Bruins, 1983), and Hamilton (Pittsburgh Penguins, 1983).

G. Both won **Coach of the Year** honors in both the IHL and AHL before becoming coach of the Flyers. Fred Shero was IHL Coach of the Year in 1960-61 with the St. Paul Saints and in the AHL in 1969-70 with the Buffalo Bisons. Bob McCammon was honored once in the IHL with the Port Huron Flags in 1975-76 and twice in the AHL with the Maine Mariners in 1977-78 and 1980-81.

H. Both McCammon and Rose were born on the same day, **April 14, 1941.**

I. Both Dr. Gregg and Dr. Medich have M.D. degrees and are qualified **physicians.**

J. All played at one time or another for the **Johnstown Jets.** The Jets were the model for the movie "SLAPSHOT" which was filmed in the Pennsylvania town in the Jets' home rink, the Cambria County Veterans Memorial Auditorium. Dave Hanson and Steve Carlson played two of the three "Hansen brothers" who were major characters in the film, made in 1976.

K. All were **original-roster** players with the WHA in that league's first season in 1972-73. Green, Pleau, Cunniff, and Ley played for New England; Parent and Polano for Philadelphia; Cheevers for Cleveland; and Sutherland for Winnipeg.

L. Both won the **Conn Smythe Trophy** as MVP in the Stanley Cup play-offs while playing for the **losing** finalist. Crozier won the award in 1966 as a member of the Detroit Red Wings, while Hall won it in 1968 with the St. Louis Blues.

M. Each has won the **Lester Patrick Trophy** presented for "contributions to hockey in the United States." All were great players for U.S.-based teams, except for Schulz who is the well-known cartoonist and creator of "PEANUTS." Schultz has long been active in amateur hockey in the United States both as a recreational player and supporter of the game.

N. All four are **lawyers.**

O. Each has a CHL trophy named after him.

P. Each has **assisted Gordie Howe** score at least one goal in the NHL. Delvecchio is at the top of the list with 210 assists, followed by Lindsay (147), and Kelly (84). Wilson, Allen, Talbot, and Berenson had one each. A total of 131 players assisted Howe in scoring his 801 NHL goals being credited with 1,239 assists. Howe scored 786 goals with Detroit between 1946 and 1971, and 15 with Hartford in 1979-80.

Q. Each of these five goalies gave up over **fifty goals** to **Gordie Howe** in their careers. Worsley gave up the most—70—of which 11 were with Montreal, 58 with the New York Rangers, and one with Minnesota. Lumley gave up 60—8 with Boston, 28 with Toronto, and 24 with Chicago. Plante gave up 54—42 with Montreal, 10 with New York, and 2 with St. Louis. Rollins gave up 53—44 with Chicago, 9 with Toronto. Bower gave up 50—37 with Toronto, 13 with New York. Howe scored his 801 regular season NHL goals against a total of 66 different goalies.

R. All suffered injury to or loss of an **eye** but remained in the game in one capacity or another. Bastien, a goalie, became a coach and GM in the AHL and NHL while Parent returned to the Philadelphia Flyers after an eye injury in 1979 as the goalie coach. Neeld lost an eye playing junior hockey but continued to play professionally in the NAHL and IHL. Chadwick became an NHL referee and is now a member of the Hall of Fame. Sonmor became a college coach and later coached in the WHA and NHL.

S. All three played professional lacrosse.

T. These three men are the only players in the **Toronto Maple Leaf's** history to have worn **#27**. Nykoluk, who was named Leafs coach on January 10, 1981, wore it first when he played 32 games for the Leafs in 1956-57. Mahovlich got it the next year and carried it until 1968. Sittler got the number in 1970 and wore it until traded to Philadelphia on January 20, 1982.

U. All three goalies earned **shut outs** in their **first NHL starts.** Thomas shut out the Vancouver Canucks as a member of the Montreal Canadiens on January 14, 1973. The Los Angeles Kings' Lessard whitewashed Buffalo, 6-0, at the Forum on October 26, 1978, and Moore, a free agent walk-on with the Philadelphia Flyers in 1978, made his first NHL start against the Colorado Rockies at the Spectrum on March 6, 1979, and shut them out 5-0.

V. During the seven-year period from 1976-77 to 1982-83, these seven teams have been a "parent club" to the AHL **Springfield Indians.** During that period of time the team has changed its colors, uniforms, and logos five times, and has played in two different buildings, the Big "E" Coliseum and the Springfield Civic Center.

W. Each team was **coached** to one or more play-off championships by **Fred Shero.** He won the Turner Cup with St. Paul (1959-60; 1960-61), the Adams Cup with St. Paul (1964-65) and Omaha (1970-71), the Calder Cup with Buffalo (1969-70), and the Stanley Cup with Philadelphia (1973-74; 1974-75). He also won the 1957-58 Quebec Professional Hockey League play-off championship with Shawinigan, as well as ten regular-season championships during his coaching career.

X. All were **original-roster** players with the 1967 NHL expansion **Pittsburgh Penguins.**

Y. Between 1971 and 1979, Collyard and Brooks were linemates for seven of eight seasons with **six different teams** in five leagues. They first played together with the CHL Kansas City Blues, followed by the Fort Worth Texans (CHL), St. Louis Blues (NHL), Denver Spurs (WHL), and Philadelphia Firebirds (NAHL and AHL).

Z. Each of these twelve players was traded at one time or another in their careers for veteran center Walt McKechnie. The Toronto Maple Leafs drafted McKechnie as a sixteen-year-old in the first round of the 1963 amateur draft and traded him to the WHL Phoenix Roadrunners for Steve Witiuk on October 15, 1967. On February 17, 1968, the Minnesota North Stars acquired him from Phoenix for Bob Charlebois, and traded him (with Joey Johnston) to the California Golden Seals on May 20, 1971 for Dennis Hextall. The New York Rangers acquired him in the Intra-League Draft on June 10, 1974, and traded him two days later to the Boston Bruins for Derek Sanderson. Boston in turn traded him to the Detroit Red Wings (along with a 1975 third round draft pick) on February 18, 1975 for Hank Nowak and Earl Anderson. Acquired by the Washington Capitals along with two future draft picks for the Caps' 1979 3rd round pick (Boris Fistric) and as compensation for the free agent signing of goalie Ron Low, whom the Red Wings had signed on August 17, 1977.

The Capitals traded McKechnie to the Cleveland Barons on December 9, 1977, for Bob Girard and Cleveland's 2nd round draft pick in 1978 (Paul MacKinnon). The merger of the Barons with the Minnesota North Stars on June 15, 1978, brought him back to Minnesota's organization for the second time, and they in turn sent him to the team that first drafted him in 1963, Toronto, on October 5, 1978, for the Leaf's 3rd round pick in 1980 (Randy Velischek). The Colorado Rockies acquired McKechnie on March 3, 1980, in exchange for their 3rd round pick in 1980 (Fred Boimstruck). He then became a Detroit Red Wing again on October 1, 1981, when he signed with them as a free agent and played with them through the 1982-83 season. Walter Thomas John McKechnie then returned to the North Stars (again as a free agent) for the third time in his career and was named by them as player-assistant coach of their CHL development team, the Salt Lake Golden Eagles, for the 1983-84 season.

MYSTERY PLAYER U

MYSTERY PLAYER V

PART IX

MYSTERY PLAYER W

"BIG HORNS," "BUCKAROOS" & "BLUEBIRDS". . .ICE CHIPS III

Here is our third set of questions about the odds and ends of hockey.

1 Where do (or did) the following twenty-six professional or junior teams play, and in what leagues?

A. Big Horns	N. Fincups
B. Castors (Beavers)	O. Whoopies
C. Goaldiggers	P. Aeros
D. Six Guns	Q. Roamers
E. Komets	R. Freedoms
F. Remparts	S. Buckaroos
G. Toros	T. Millionaires
H. Bulls	U. Robins
I. Seagulls	V. Firebirds
J. Bluebirds	W. South Stars
K. Dixie Flyers	X. Bombers
L. Express	Y. Rustlers
M. Alpines	Z. Thistles

2 We list below the names of the sixteen winners of the NHL Calder Memorial Trophy for Rookie of the Year from the expansion year of 1967-68 to 1982-83. From what amateur team did each come to the NHL?

A. Derek Sanderson (1968)	I. Bryan Trottier (1976)
B. Danny Grant (1969)	J. Willi Plett (1977)
C. Tony Esposito (1970)	K. Mike Bossy (1978)
D. Gilbert Perreault (1971)	L. Bobby Smith (1979)
E. Ken Dryden (1972)	M. Ray Bourque (1980)
F. Steve Vickers (1973)	N. Peter Stastny (1981)
G. Denis Potvin (1974)	O. Dale Hawerchuk (1982)
H. Eric Vail (1975)	P. Steve Larmer (1983)

MYSTERY PLAYER X

3 What was the last year that the Olympic or World's Hockey Championship was won by a team that was not the National Team of the country which they represented, and what was the name of that championship team?

4 What title did the Boston Olympics, later a long-time member of the Eastern Amateur Hockey League, win in 1933?

5 The Stanley Cup has been played for every year since it was donated by Lord Stanley of Preston in 1893. While there has been a play-off for it every year, there was no winner or presentation in one of those years. What year was it not awarded and why?

6 The Philadelphia Flyers had to overcome two unusual obstacles to win their second consecutive Stanley Cup championship in 1975. What were they?

7 The New York Islanders have certainly proved their ability to play under pressure with their consecutive Stanley Cup wins in the early 1980's. But the most pressure that they, or any other team, was forced to play under over an entire play-off came a number of years before their first Cup victory. What NHL record did the Islanders' establish for "playing under pressure" before ever winning a Cup?

8 Since its founding in 1946 through the 1983-84 season, a total of fifty-one different teams have played in the International Hockey League. Of those, ten have represented the Detroit-Windsor area. What were their names?

9 Within ten, how many scoreless (0-0) ties were played in the NHL through the 1982-83 season, and which team has been involved in the most scoreless ties over its history?

10 Two of the biggest trades in NHL history occured just over a year apart. One took place between Chicago and Boston on May 15, 1967, and the other involved Detroit and Toronto on March 3, 1968. Who were the thirteen players included in these two deals?

11 Who was the last player/head coach in the NHL, a practice no longer permitted under NHL rules?

12 Bobby Orr was the highest scoring defenseman in NHL history both in total points (915) and average points-per-game (1.393), but he does not hold the record for points in a game by a blueliner. Who does, and how many points did this defenseman collect in his record-setting game?

MYSTERY PLAYER Y

MYSTERY PLAYER Z

ICE CHIPS III. . . ANSWERS

1 Here are the home cities and leagues of our twenty-six teams:

A. **Billings, MT** (WHL Jrs.)
B. **Sherbrooke, PQ** (QMJHL Jrs.)
C. **Toledo, OH** (IHL)
D. **Albuquerque, NM** (CHL)
E. **Ft. Wayne, IN** (IHL)

F. **Quebec City, PQ** (QMJHL Jrs.)
G. **Toronto, Ontario** (WHA)

H. **Birmingham, AL** (WHA, CHL)
I. **Atlantic City, NJ** (EHL)

J. **Johnstown, PA** (EHL)

K. **Nashville, TN** (EHL)

L. **Fredericton, NB** (AHL)

M. **Moncton, NB** (AHL)

N. **Hamilton, Ontario** (OHA Jrs.)
O. **Macon, GA** (SHL)
P. **Houston, TX** (WHA)
Q. **Lake Placid, NY** (EHL)
R. **Concord and Manchester, NH** (NEHL)
S. **Portland, OR** (WHL)
T. **Vancouver, BC** (1915 Stanley Cup winner)
U. **Richmond, VA** (AHL)
V. **Philadelphia, PA** (NAHL, AHL); Syracuse, NY (AHL)
W. **Nashville, TN and Birmingham, AL** (CHL)
X. **Flin Flon, Manitoba** (WHL Jrs.)
Y. **Red Deer, Alberta** (AJHL Jrs.); **Tucson, AZ** (PHL)
Z. **Kenora, Ontario** (1907 Stanley Cup winner)

2 The sixteen Calder Trophy winners from 1968 to 1983 played their amateur hockey with: .

A. **Niagara Falls Flyers** (OHA)
B. **Peterborough PTPS** (OHA)
C. **Michigan Tech University** (WCHA)
D. **Montreal Jr. Canadiens** (OHA)
E. **Cornell University** (ECAC)
F. **Toronto Marlboros** (OHA)
G. **Ottawa 67's** (OHA)
H. **Sudbury Wolves** (OHA)

I. **Lethbridge Broncos** (WHL Jrs.)
J. **St. Catherines Black Hawks** (OHA)
K. **Laval Nationals** (QMJHL)
L. **Ottawa 67's** (OHL)
M. **Verdun Black Hawks** (QMJHL)
N. **Slovan Bratislava**
O. **Cornwall Royals** (QMJHL)
P. **Niagara Falls Flyers** (OHL)

3 The 1961 World Hockey Championships were held in Geneva, Switzerland, and the tournament was won by the team representing Canada—the **Trail (B.C.) Smoke Eaters.** It was the 19th, and last, time it was won by a Canadian team.

4 The Boston Olympics were the only U.S. team to ever win the **World Championship** (other than the 1960 Olympic team) when it captured the title in Prague in 1933. (Since 1972 there have been separate World Tournaments in Olympic years. Prior to that, the Olympic champion was also considered the World champion.)

5 In 1919, the Montreal Canadiens traveled to Seattle, WA, to play the PCHL champion Seattle Metropolitans for the Cup. The series was halted after five games (tied a 2-2-1), however, by the Seattle Department of Health because of the **influenza** epidemic and the death from the disease of Joe Hall.

6 The Flyers had to overcome not only the challenge of the Buffalo Sabres to win the 1975 Stanley Cup, but also **fog** and **bats.** In Buffalo, the heat and humidity of a warm May plus over 16,000 people in the non-air conditioned Memorial Auditorium mixed with the cold surface of the ice to produce a thick layer of fog. It required frequent stoppages of play to allow rink attendants to skate around with towels to dissipate the opaque whiteness. Another game was delayed by a low-flying bat which continuously circled the heads of the players as they tried to concentrate on the game. Sabre center Jim Lorentz finally dispatched the unwelcome visitor while awaiting a face-off by striking it down in mid-flight with his stick. Flyer center Rick MacLeish then carried the unfortunate deceased to the penalty box.

7 **Eight** times during the 1975 play-offs, the Islanders won games which, if they had lost, would have **eliminated** them from further Cup action. They faced elimination in the third game of the best-of-three series with the New York Rangers, defeated the Pittsburgh Penguins in seven games after losing the first three of the series, and then won the fourth, fifth, and sixth games of their semi-final series against the defending Stanley Cup champion Philadelphia Flyers after losing the first three games of that series as well. They lost their ninth "no tomorrow" game as the Flyers clinched the series in the seventh game and went on to defeat the Buffalo Sabres for the Cup. No other team in Stanley Cup history staved off elimination eight times in a single play-off year.

8 Detroit has been represented in the IHL by teams called the **Auto Club, Jerry Lynch, Bright's Goodyears,** and **Metal Moldings.** Its Canadian neighbor, Windsor, Ontario, located just across the Detroit River, was represented by the **Staffords, Spitfires, Hettche Spitfires, Ryancretes,** and **Bulldogs.**

9 Through the 1982-83 season, there were **140** scoreless (0-0) ties played in NHL history. The **Boston Bruins** have played the most, 33, followed closely by the Chicago Black Hawks with 32.

10 The first "Trade of the Century" came on May 15, 1967, when the Chicago Black Hawks sent **Phil Esposito, Fred Stanfield,** and **Ken Hodge** to the Boston Bruins for **Pit Martin, Gilles Marotte,** and **Jack Norris.** (Esposito was involved in another big trade on November 7, 1975, when the Bruins sent him along with defenseman Carol Vadnais to the New York Rangers for Brad Park, Jean Ratelle, and Joe Zanussi.)

The second blockbuster trade took place on March 3, 1968, when the Toronto Maple Leafs sent **Frank Mahovlich, Garry Unger, Pete Stemkowski,** and the rights to **Carl Brewer** to the Detroit Red Wings for **Paul Henderson, Norm Ullman,** and **Floyd Smith.** Mahovlich had scored 285 goals in his eleven and one-half seasons with the Leafs, and Unger would later become both the NHL's all-time "Ironman" (appearing in 914 consecutive games over eleven years) and a 400+ goal scorer. Henderson became the hero of the 1972 Canada-USSR series, and Smith later returned to the Leafs as their coach.

11 **Doug Harvey** served the New York Rangers as player/head coach in 1961-62.

12 Defenseman **Tom Bladon** of the Philadelphia Flyers collected eight points in a game on December 11, 1977, with four goals and four assists in an 11-1 Flyer victory over the Cleveland Barons at the Spectrum in Philadelphia.

MYSTERY PLAYER

NHL GM's & COACHES . . . . PHOTO IDENTIFICATIONS

Here are the identities of the twenty-six current or recent NHL GMs, head coaches or assistant coaches who are shown throughout the book in their early playing careers in the minor leagues. (The minor league team they are shown with follows each man's name.)

A **Mike Nykoluk** (Hershey Bears)
B. Nick Polano (Providence Reds)
C. Don Cherry (Hershey Bears)
D. Fred Shero (New York Rovers)
E. Gerry Cheevers (Rochester Americans)
F. Bob McCammon (Port Huron Flags)
G. Bob Berry (Cleveland Barons)
H. Barclay Plager (Springfield Indians)
I. **Al MacNeil** (Rochester Americans)
J. **Danny Belisle** (Baltimore Clippers)
K. **Jack "Tex" Evans** (Buffalo Bisons)
L. **Terry Murray** (Baltimore Clippers)
M. Floyd Smith (Springfield Indians)
N. Al Arbour (Rochester Americans)
O. John Ferguson (Cleveland Barons)
P. **Red Berenson** (Quebec Aces)
Q. John McLellan (Cleveland Barons)
R. Red Sullivan (Hershey Bears)
S. **Parker MacDonald** (Springfield Indians)
T. **Doug Barkley** (Buffalo Bisons)
U. Ted Harris (Cleveland Barons)
V. **Fred Glover** (Cleveland Barons)
W. Mike Corrigan (Rochester Americans)
X. **Phil Maloney** (Hershey Bears)
Y. **Jean Ratelle** (Baltimore Clippers)
Z. **Ken Schinkel** (Springfield Indians)

About the Authors...

BRUCE C. COOPER

An experienced hockey writer and administrator, Bruce Cooper has written about hockey and other sports for numerous newspapers and magazines. A Philadelphia native, he is a graduate of Temple University (B.Sc., 1968) where he also did graduate work in communications. He taught English, writing, and dramatics at the William Penn Charter School in Philadelphia and was later an administrator at Haverford College in nearby Haverford, PA., before devoting full time to writing and sports administration.

He was formerly Director of Press and Public Relations for the NAHL Philadelphia Firebirds when that team was in operation, and has written most of the NHL Philadelphia Flyers' publications and yearbooks in recent years. He also wrote a popular column entitled *SCOOP* in the Flyers' program magazine, *Goal,* for a number of seasons. On a number of occasions he has collaborated with co-author Gene Hart as guest analyst on several Flyers' broadcasts.

Among his previous publications is the book *Conditioning for Ice Hockey: YEAR ROUND* (Leisure Press, 1983) which he co-authored with Flyers physical conditioning coach Pat Croce. He is also working on several other projects scheduled for future publication, including a history of the Philadelphia Flyers.

His activities as a free lance writer often take him to as many as 125 major and minor league professional, college, and amateur hockey games a season. He also serves as President of both Cooper-Clement Associates, Ardmore, PA, and Radiological Imaging Corporation, Los Angeles, CA.

GENE HART

One of the best known broadcasters in sports, Gene Hart has been the "voice" of the NHL Philadelphia Flyers since that club's inception in 1967. But his ties with the game go back to his youth, when he used to attend the Sunday afternoon double-headers at the old Madison Square Garden in the late 1930's, which featured the Eastern League's New York Rovers.

Born in New York City in 1931, he moved to Atlantic City in the early forties but still followed the Rangers and Rovers faithfully. He began his broadcasting career in Atlantic City while still in his teens as voice of the EHL Atlantic City Sea Gulls, as well as doing scholastic and collegiate sports. He also attended Trenton (NJ) State College and Temple University, where he received his degree in education. While building his broadcasting career, he also taught in the New Jersey public schools for 16 years (including a two-year "stay" in the education department at the N.J. State Prison at Leesburg.)

He returned to hockey in the mid-1950's with the EHL Jersey Devils, which played in Cherry Hill, N.J., before joining the Flyers with the NHL's expansion in 1967.

In the past seventeen years, Hart has broadcast four Stanley Cup finals, five NHL All-Star Games, and has been a guest play-by-play broadcaster on the NHL network. He has also broadcast games in the NHL-USSR series in 1976 and 1982.

This venture with Bruce Cooper is his first in the book world.

We hope that you have found this book enjoyable, and we invite both your comments and suggestions for future such projects. You may write us at:

Bruce C. Cooper
Gene Hart
P.O. Box 468
Ardmore, PA 19003-0468

SUPER HOCKEY BOOKS
From Leisure Press

Conditioning for Ice Hockey: YEAR ROUND
by PAT CROCE, LPT, ATC and BRUCE C. COOPER

THE HOCKEY DRILL BOOK
By Dr. GUY PALMER

■ ***Conditioning for Hockey: YEAR ROUND.*** Pat Croce and Bruce
C. Cooper. Techniques and programs for conditioning for hockey;
a well-illustrated guide to all aspects of fitness for hockey; written
for hockey players of all ages. 144 pages. $9.95.

■ ***The Hockey Drill Book.*** Dr. Guy Palmer, Ph.D. Over 200 illustrated
drills for hockey players of all ages. 352 pages. $14.95.

Both books are available at your local bookstore or they may be
ordered by sending a check or money order for the full amount,
plus $1.25 per book for postage and handling to:

    Leisure Press
    P.O. Box 3
    West Point, N.Y. 10996